PROFOUND SPACE

PROFOUND SPACE

3 Illusions Keeping You From The Life You Want & The Leader You Could Be

Gerd Bents, MSEd, MDiv

MCP BOOKS

MCP Books
555 Winderley Pl, Suite 225
Maitland, FL 32751
407.339.4217
www.millcitypress.net

Paperback ISBN-13: 978-1-66289-473-2
Ebook ISBN-13: 978-1-66289-474-9

To Raena & Harm

You may choose to hate your failure, or to love yourself.
But you can't choose both.

Love, Dad

Table of Contents

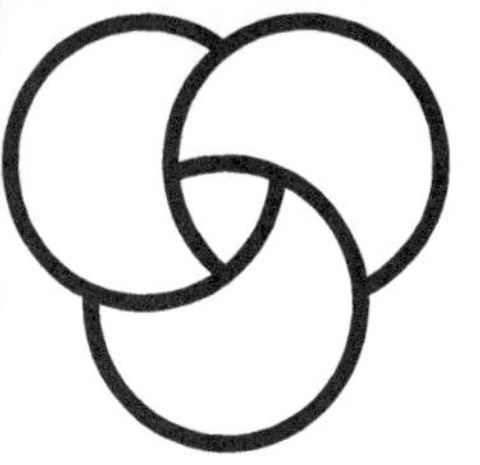

Welcome

WHEN I SAY *profound space,* I'm not talking about space shuttles and astronauts. I'm not talking about any tangible, physical space, actually.

Rather, profound space is a dynamic environment, a mind-set, a way of life where you realize personal growth. Profound space allows you to surge beyond your expectations, to achieve and succeed beyond your boundaries. It exponentially impacts your performance in every aspect of life. It allows you to deepen your relationships. It allows you to become more *you.*

I'm talking about *that* space. And it is profound.

The most important aspect of profound space is that you can *create* it, both personally and professionally. Anytime. Anywhere. Right here, right now, you, me.

In the coming chapters, we're going to push past all your preambles. We're going to resolve the three mysteries of courage, insight, and autonomy. We're going to grow a relationship. Build trust. Share thoughts. Confront challenges.

We're going to create profound space.

This book resolves mysteries that help you solve issues. That is, this book doesn't solve issues for you. It doesn't tell you what to do. Rather, it helps you think differently so you can figure out what to do. This is not a silver bullet. But it is profound.

Now, if this seems daunting, put the book aside, steady yourself, then come back another day. This is work, and it isn't easy. It's best to be prepared.

If you're ready, you will grow beyond measure. You will accomplish your goals. You will discover clarity and focus and energy beyond what you would otherwise experience. You will create profound space.

So, are you ready?

Welcome to *Profound Space*. Let's do this.

Preamble

IN GRADUATE SCHOOL, a mentor told me never to read preambles to books. "They're bullshit," he said. I believed him at the time.

Today I disagree. I always read preambles. They may be bullshit, but they're bullshit that guards something. Something deeper. Something more.

Preambles guard profound space.

Beyond Grasping

When I was eighteen, my father sensed I was destined for a service profession that interacted profoundly with the personal lives of great people. So he spoke words I will never forget: "Gerd, always remember one thing: the issue is never the issue. There is always something more."

THE ISSUE IS NEVER THE ISSUE. THERE IS ALWAYS SOMETHING MORE.

I have never forgotten.

I serve as a consultant, coach, trusted advisor, confidant, and sometimes hired friend for people who set out to achieve their visions. I serve people who want to grow. Often, these are accomplished, intelligent, complex, and action-oriented professionals. By all means, people who perform at high levels. They aren't perfect, but they're focused on growth.

In addition to my work with individuals, I also work with organizations, corporations, and businesses. Having consulted with over a hundred organizations, I've been able to distinguish the mindsets and thinking patterns that increase capacity for growth, team unity, and ultimately success.

As I continue to work with organizations and individuals in complex situations, I remember my father's words: *The issue is never the issue.* His wisdom brings to light what we often take for granted—that each of us is much deeper, much more complex, and much more robust than what we choose to present to the world. We are each more profound than we let on.

In other words, we all have preambles. Including me. Including you.

Preambles often come in the form of simple deflection: sarcasm, disingenuous emotion, distracting surface-level stories. Preambles are the stories before a story that lead you where the storyteller wants you to go. But preambles serve to avoid personal boundaries, create self-limiting thoughts, and replace true vulnerability with routine anger. As my mentor said, they're bullshit.

But if we push past these preambles, we'll discover something deeper behind the scenes. We'll find ourselves face-to-face with powerful mysteries to resolve, and we'll eventually find ourselves face-to-face with profound space.

This is why I've made it my practice to listen to people's preambles first, but then listen more deeply. I try to listen beyond the preamble. And try to help people push past these preambles because the issue is never the issue. There's always something more.

In my years working with people, I've seen some people learn to grow while others continue to grasp.

Those who grow are the ones who get beyond their preambles. They become better at what they do and better at who they are. They become more congruent with themselves. They increase their capacity for change. They advance in their careers and move their visions forward. They become adept at finding fulfillment in their life.

On the contrary, those who lead a life of grasping hold firm to the very preambles they construct. Their preambles tell whatever story they want the world to believe. They turn a deaf ear to the deeper truth locked behind the stories they tell others and themselves. These people routinely fail at their achievements, make excuses for their performance, and alter their desired course at the first sign of adversity.

They grasp for confidence but live in fear. They grasp for joy but remain unfulfilled. They grasp for understanding but find very few pleasing answers. They grasp for growth but remain . . . well, grasping.

Profound space is the remedy for a life of grasping.

How do I know? Because I've helped hundreds of people push beyond preambles, resolve their mysteries, and embrace profound space.

And because I've done it myself.

My Cigar Box

The Preamble

On my dresser is a small cigar box I discovered during my travels. It isn't necessarily special, but it's functional.

Inside this cigar box, I keep four items:

1. A pearl tie clip worn by my grandfather. My grandmother gave it to me long after his death. I've never worn it. But it's nice to have something of a man I know only through stories.
2. A set of cuff links I wear maybe once a year. Maybe.
3. An old torn bandana that belonged to my youngest brother, Max. He died when he was thirty-five. I used to travel with the bandana as a reminder of Max's adventurous spirit. But then I got a tattoo in his honor, so now I feel the bandana can stay home.
4. Magnetic metal collar tabs I wear daily with my dress shirts.

Like the box itself, none of these items are special to me or necessary. None of them. In fact, they're clutter. And I hate clutter.

One by one, these items came into my life. I didn't know what to do with them. I didn't want them just lying around, for fear they may get lost, damaged, or, quite frankly, laughed at. But I also didn't want to get rid of them. That seemed brash, cold, heartless.

So, one by one, I simply swept the items into the cigar box. It seemed like a convenient space to keep these things of seemingly little value.

That's what I told myself, anyway.

But over time, this convenient space has taken on a life of its own. It's become something more . . . because of those damn collar tabs.

Let me explain.

Every day, I wear a collared shirt to work, and I use the magnetic tabs to ensure my collar looks sharp. It's part of my morning routine of getting dressed and feeling prepared.

Which means that every day, I open the cigar box.

Every day, I acknowledge my grandfather's tie clip and wonder how often he actually wore it.

Every day, I look at the cuff links, rolling my eyes and wondering why I even have a French cuff shirt. Seriously.

Every day, I see Max's red bandana and ask myself what I can learn from his life that might benefit me and others today.

Every—single—day.

This cigar box has started to define my morning routine. It's started to define my thoughts. It's even started to define me.

Which means this isn't the full story, the *real* story, about my cigar box.

It's only the preamble.

Beyond the Preamble

In the preamble, I told you it's nice to have my grandfather's tie clip; it's something from a man I only know through stories told.

But here, beyond the preamble, I'll tell you the clip represents an intimidating truth: that my example and my words hold more power than I may fully understand. It reminds me that how I treat my children today will have repercussions tomorrow and for generations to come. The stories told of me long beyond my years and long out of my control will set expectations for grandchildren and great-grandchildren. The clip is a tangible weight of the tension I carry between fear and responsibility—in the shape of a pearl.

In the preamble, I told you my cuff links are completely unnecessary.

But here, beyond the preamble, I'll tell you they reflect my continual struggle between frivolity and function. They remind me that some things are unnecessary yet also adorning, and that some possessions have very little meaning yet bring small joy. They remind me of my growing edge: my struggle with setting boundaries around what I want versus what I need.

In the preamble, I told you my brother's bandana is a nice but largely unnecessary memento.

But here, beyond the preamble, I'll tell you that it's a pain-filled joy. It's a small and tangible piece from Max's complex life. It bears a hint of broken relationships, unreconciled imperfection, destructive secrets. It challenges me to live today because tomorrow is uncertain. It confronts me with how I live my life, because life may be short, and opportunities may be lost.

As you can see, my cigar box is more than just a convenient place where I've tossed a handful of nonessential items. Much more. It holds great meaning and great power for me.

It represents my profound space.

But I didn't realize that until I pushed beyond all those preambles—and until I learned how to unlock the mysteries of courage, insight, and autonomy.

Opening my cigar box isn't exactly easy. Magnets lock the lid. More strongly than you might think. I have to pry apart the magnets with both hands moving in opposite directions.

I do this every morning, every time I wish to enter the cigar box. Again, because of those damn collar tabs.

I've learned that profound space is locked too. Not with magnets but with mysteries: courage, insight, and autonomy.

On the surface, these three concepts don't seem that mysterious. They seem straightforward.

But in truth, courage, insight, and autonomy aren't what they seem. They're paradoxes. The way many of us understand them is misguided, if not outright incorrect.

The confusion lies in the stories the world tells us about ourselves. The world tells us we need confidence, when we actually need courage. It tells us we need information, when we actually need insight. And it tells us we need freedom, when we actually need autonomy.

In simpler terms, the world says "Fake it till you make it," "Knowledge is power," and "Free yourself." At best, that's a partial story. At worst, it's an outright lie.

COURAGE, INSIGHT, AND AUTONOMY AREN'T WHAT THEY SEEM. THEY'RE PARADOXES. THE WAY MANY OF US UNDERSTAND THEM IS MISGUIDED, IF NOT OUTRIGHT INCORRECT.

And so I leaned in. I began to wrestle with these mysteries of courage, insight, and autonomy. I began to see that each is powerful in its own right but even more so when combined with the others. I began to see that each presented an illusion, a challenge, and finally a resolution.

Resolving these mysteries allowed me to unlock the door to profound space. And what I found in there is more important than collar tabs.

Courage, insight, and autonomy are the keys to profound space for me, for you, for teams, and for organizations. So we're going to resolve these mysteries together. We're going to unlock *your* cigar box. And we're going to see what's so important in there.

We're going to enter your profound space.

But first, please allow me to share one more story with you—the story of why I wrote this book.

Finding Yourself

Have you ever watched a seasoned fly-angler casting upstream into a riffle at twenty yards? It is beautiful to behold.

A seasoned angler appears to be a natural participant in the backdrop of the event, the fly rod like a magical wand, waving into existence an artwork of swirling mystery, willing its results from the living stream.

The keen observer can witness the intricate detail of each movement. The twitch of the thumb. The break of the elbow. The loaded rod. The looped line. The glance of the eyes. The release. The placement. The mending. The stripping.

The beauty that lies in the sequence of those tiny, little details. Together, those movements create a swirling mystery of trial and error, time and intensity, failure and persistence, discipline and discovery.

To walk along a stream and observe seasoned fly-casters is to witness a life of dedication to that mystery.

TOGETHER, THE MOVEMENTS CREATE A SWIRLING MYSTERY OF TRIAL AND ERROR, TIME AND INTENSITY, FAILURE AND PERSISTENCE, DISCIPLINE AND DISCOVERY.

The novices are noticeable, too, with less magic and very little mystery. The novice looks like a confused spectator, standing in cold water, swinging a stick. Case in point, I still, after sixteen years, look like one of those very people, standing in cold water, swinging a stick.

Expertise takes intentional time.

The thing is, successful fly fishing often has very little to do with finding fish and a whole lot to do with finding yourself.

Luckily for me, Randy was the perfect coach.

Randy began teaching me to fly-fish in 2007. Built tall, with trim gray hair and fitter than the average baby boomer, he was nearing the evening of his career and was escorting his six daughters—one by one—into adult life. Yet he himself wasn't finished growing.

He had a strong desire to learn, to explore new ideas, to experience the world in new ways, to challenge what he traditionally believed, to become something more. He combined his learned skepticism with a simple curiosity. This combination allowed him not to succumb to pessimism. Instead, he maintained a healthy engagement in life. He routinely sought to discover the best in other people as well as uncover the best of himself.

So Randy began guiding me, his early-thirties understudy, in the art of fly-fishing. Moreover, he began guiding me in the mystery of the fly-anglers' dedication. I thought I was just learning logistics—tying knots, cutting snags, casting. Actually, I was learning something extremely profound.

Our first lesson was on the Kinnickinnic River, just outside of River Falls, Wisconsin. I was frustrated—and letting it show. If I'd been fishing for sixty minutes, I'd no doubt spent fifty-six of them out of the water, cutting snags and tying new knots and flies.

Typically, Randy would be in the water, right alongside me. But when I snagged my line once again, he took my rod, handed me his, then headed for the bank. He sat right down and got to work fixing my line.

But in the few minutes it took him to fix my rod, I snagged the other. So we traded again.

And so it went. We kept handing rods back and forth. He was my personal snag-removal service, always ready to tend to my mistakes and give me a ready-to-go line in the meantime. He made certain I was focused on the mystery of casting; I made certain he didn't get a chance to fish.

While his fingers deftly handled those snags and knots, his eyes would peer over his reading glasses, keeping a close watch on my progress. Even from the bank, he had a knack for knowing when to speak up and offer guidance and when to be quiet and allow me to work it out myself. We were in sync that way—the beginnings of a friendship with a deep understanding.

As the frustration faded, I began to find my rhythm. Eventually, I felt a tug on the other end of the line. I had my first fish! I was elated!

But Randy's elation exponentially outweighed mine. He jumped up, rushed into the water, and coached me on how to land the fish without hurting it. And when I did just that, fifty-five-year-old Randy sat on the bank, laughing and cheering and giggling with a childlike joy I found just as intriguing as the beautiful brown trout itself.

We fished for another hour. I caught a couple more fish. Randy, though, didn't cast a line. He just watched, coached, and celebrated.

As we hiked back to the truck, we debriefed on everything I'd learned that day. Then he said something I will never forget.

"You know, I have almost as much fun watching other people catch fish as I do catching them myself."

I believed him.

Randy not only *wanted* me to succeed; he delighted in helping me get there. He celebrated my victories as if they were his own. In a very real way, they were his victories too.

Of all the lessons I learned that day, only one stuck with me. It wasn't casting. It wasn't tying flies. It wasn't catch and release. Instead, it was *Find joy in helping others succeed.*

It stuck with me because it made me realize that's what I'm built for.

You see, this isn't a story about fly-fishing, after all. It's a story about success.

And success isn't about discovering fish. It's about discovering yourself.

I want *you* to succeed.

I want you to flourish in whatever endeavor you pursue.

I want you to reach that height, quit that bad habit, learn that new skill, get in that shape, cross that finish line, earn that elevated position—and more.

I want you to cast a vision so deep and so grand and so clear you can almost smell it, taste it, and touch it. And then

I want you to turn that vision into reality so you *truly* can smell it, taste it, and touch it.

I want you to grow—and that means changing.

I want you to become the person you've always wanted to become. I want you to be the person you know you are.

I want you to do all this without losing yourself, without making needless sacrifices, and without regrets.

I'll say it again: I want you to succeed. More importantly, I want you to be fulfilled. I want you to succeed at being *you*. That's what I'm built to do.

That's what this book is built to do too. To help you succeed. To help you find yourself. To help you move beyond preambles and resolve the three mysteries of profound space.

So let's get started.

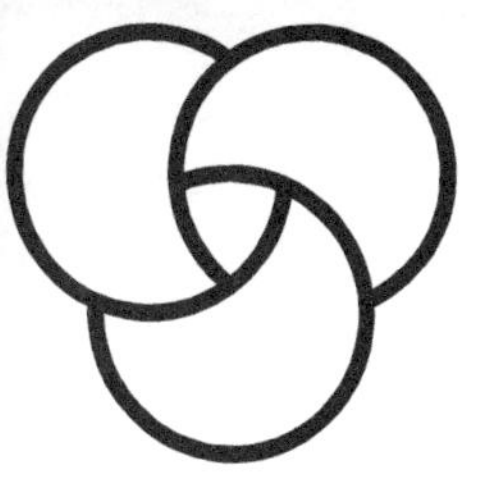

Resolving the Mystery of Courage

WE ARE CREATING profound space. To do so, we must resolve the mystery of courage. Like each of the three mysteries, courage bears three components: an illusion, a challenge, and eventually a resolution.

But there's something unique about the mystery of courage that distinguishes it from the other two. Compared to the mysteries of insight and autonomy, the mystery of courage is cloaked with emotion.

This may come as a surprise. Most of us think of courage in terms of strength, determination, grit, and a "no fear" attitude. We often believe that in order to be courageous, we must push aside or even deny our emotions.

But the Latin root of the word *courage* means "heart." There's an emotionality to courage. A vulnerability, even. There's no getting around it. Therefore, it's not a surprise that the most courageous people are those who excel at managing their own emotions.

So let's solve the mystery of courage.

1) The Illusion: Confidence
2) The Challenge: Fear
3) The Resolution: Action

The Illusion: Confidence

Confidence is overrated and often even problematic. Confidence can cause us to have a rosy vision about our potential outcomes, which can then lead us to make poorly discerned decisions.

This is partly because we conflate confidence with ideas such as "fake it till you make it." We assume that so long as we act confident, things will just turn out.

In truth, these are lies we tell ourselves in order to feel something euphoric.

Or to avoid our feelings of fear.

Gambling with Confidence

Manny made his inside bet at the roulette table. He liked inside bets. He felt they gave him a better chance to spread his wagers around. A little like diversification.

And sure enough, his plan was working. He was on a small hot streak. His previous five placements had put him $2,500 over the house. He was feeling confident.

Between spins, Manny joked with the croupier, explaining how he'd never planned to gamble. He and his friends Mark and Josh were merely in Las Vegas to see a show. But on their way to dinner, Manny decided to try his hand at the wheel. He'd expected to play only a spin or two—but now here he was, riding high.

The next spin, he lost. But then he won big on the following spin. Now he was up $3,600.

Mark and Josh went nuts. They couldn't believe what they were witnessing. They were even more excited than Manny.

But then, in the middle of his heater, Manny held up his hands. "I better take my money and run," he said with a laugh. And so he pulled his chips.

Mark and Josh trash-talked him a little about throwing in the towel. But as they headed to dinner, and as the adrenaline wore off, they all agreed that Manny had made a good decision.

A rare decision. Most people get swept up in the momentum of a hot streak, only to keep betting. But not Manny. He was feeling cool, collected, and confident.

The guys ate dinner at the casino. Manny's treat, of course. During dinner, Mark spilled his drink on his shirt, which meant they needed to make a quick detour before heading to the show. They planned to regroup in twenty minutes.

So Mark made a beeline for the hotel. Josh ducked into a quiet corner and called his wife to check in. And Manny decided he'd play a couple more spins at the table. After all, he was up $3,600 (minus the dinner tab). He had a foolproof betting strategy. He was still feeling confident.

Twenty minutes later, Mark and Josh made their way to the roulette table, where they found Manny.

He was down.

Way down.

He'd lost it all.

Manny wasn't feeling confident anymore.

Let me say that again: Manny wasn't feeling confident anymore. *Feeling.*

Confidence is a feeling, a sensation, a sensory experience. A very pleasurable experience, of course. It's invigorating. Euphoric! It's a gust of energy and much-needed motivation.

Who doesn't want to feel that way? No wonder we think confidence is the key to success. No wonder the world makes us believe we'll get that raise or accomplish that goal if only we have more confidence.

CONFIDENCE IS A FEELING, A SENSATION, A SENSORY EXPERIENCE . . . YOU CAN'T CONTROL IT.

But that's an illusion.

You don't need confidence to succeed. In fact, it may even hurt you.

Like all feelings, confidence is an internal reaction, a response. It's a byproduct of a successful event, not a predecessor to it. Yet so many people wait around, thinking they're supposed to feel confident before even beginning an endeavor. That's like waiting for bigger muscles before starting a strength-training routine.

And because confidence is a reaction, a byproduct, you can't control it. You can't make yourself feel it. You can't conjure it out of thin air. Instead, you have to grow it over time and with experience.

For example, if you're uncomfortable with public speaking, you probably won't feel confident when you begin your first presentation. And telling yourself to "just feel confident" won't do anything but draw more attention to how unconfident you feel.

Likewise, telling yourself to "act confident" will only help for a little while. Before you know it, that feeling will wear off, right while you're standing on stage in front of two hundred people. And how will *that* make you feel?

You can't force confidence, but it will grow as you experience success. Maybe you'll start to feel it when you get a few minutes into your presentation without any flubs. Or maybe you won't gain confidence until you've delivered five presentations.

You may not "feel confident" during all that time, but you will be learning. You will be dedicating yourself to a practice of action-reflection that will help you to grow. (Stay tuned for more about that later in the book.) By the time you walk up for your sixth presentation, you will have grown genuine confidence.

In other words, confidence follows success, not the other way around.

It's important to note, too, that the confidence you feel after six successful presentations is different from the confidence you feel after six successful spins at the roulette table. One confidence is based on learning and developing knowledge or skill. The other is based on coincidence, being the recipient of happenstance. That is, luck doesn't develop genuine confidence.

Case in point, Manny was riding high on euphoric confidence when he sat down at the table that second time. He'd convinced himself that confidence was all he needed to win big again. He was so convinced, in fact, that he kept pressing on, even as more and more of his chips disappeared. By the time Manny's money was gone, his confidence was too. In his case, confidence actually *impeded* success.

The point is, you don't need confidence to get ahead. You don't need confidence to finish a project. You don't need confidence to tackle a large undertaking. You don't need confidence to succeed. You don't need confidence to create profound space.

You just don't.

You need *courage*.

Let's Turn This Ship Around

Confidence is not the same as courage. Whereas confidence is a fleeting emotional reaction, courage is something more permanent. More reliable. More intentional. More useful. Confidence is the end result. But courage is with you at the beginning. Confidence you must learn. But courage you can control.

On April 15, 1912, Arthur Rostron was captaining the RMS *Carpathia,* a passenger steamship, when he received an SOS about the *Titanic*'s fatal disaster.

The *Carpathia* was sixty miles away from the scene, with nothing but darkness and dangerous ice floes between them. Other ships were closer to the *Titanic* but overcome with fear. They refused to respond.

The moment Rostron received the SOS, he made a monumental decision. "Mr. Dean," he said to his first officer, "turn this ship around." He risked his life and the lives of his crew in order to come the *Titanic*'s aid.

His decision saved over seven hundred people from imminent death.

Did Captain Rostron feel confident when he made this decision? Most likely, he felt the opposite of confidence: fear. But he was determined to face the challenge, and he made the decision to take action and do what the situation called for.

There was another captain who made a different decision that same night. Captain Stanley Lord of the SS *Californian* had a decision of his own to make. Though controversy surrounds what truly happened aboard the *Californian,* the final decision was to ignore the flares of the *Titanic*'s SOS calls from a mere twenty miles away.

The *Californian* had the capability and the capacity to rescue all 2,240 passengers off the Titanic. If they had only had the courage to turn *their* ship around. Instead, 1,500 people died that night.

Why did one captain act one way and the other respond differently? Did one have more confidence than the other? Maybe. Maybe not.

Surely, both captains faced a fearful decision, regardless of how much confidence they felt. Both captains had an opportunity to come to the aid of the *Titanic* and save thousands of lives. Both captains had a difficult decision mired in unimaginable risk.

So what moved Rostron, but not Lord, to act?

Courage.

Courage is the willingness to do what is necessary in the midst of a challenge. Rostron had courage to act in the face of challenge.

And that challenge is fear.

The Challenge: Fear

There are many obstacles and challenges to creating profound space. But one obstacle stands out above the rest. The most powerful obstacle is fear. More specifically, your mind's inability to understand and cope with fear.

FEAR IS YOUR ONLY REAL ENEMY. AN ENEMY THAT, LARGELY, YOU CREATE.

Fear is your only real enemy. An enemy that, largely, you create. You create it by the perfectionism you assume, the procrastination you employ, the attitude you choose, the apathy you succumb to, the negative self-talk you listen to—all of it is your creation.

But what you create you can also control. You can get under it. You can understand it. You can eliminate it.

If fear is the most powerful *obstacle,* then the ability to control that fear is the most powerful *tool.* When you learn the nuances of courage, you will unlock your ability to overcome fear—you will be able to take the right action in the midst of fear.

The first step is to realize that fear doesn't have to be that powerful.

How Real Is Fear?

He wrapped the sheet and blanket snug over his head and around his body, leaving only his small face peeking out. Even that discomforting offering was a risk, but one worth taking so he could keep an eye on the room around him.

His bed he had pushed into the corner, positioning the two windows at his back and behind his head, respectively. He lay on his right side, with his head tilted toward the door, away from the windows. The shades were drawn. If they looked in his window, he thought, at least they couldn't see his face.

They *knew*. The police. They *knew* it was him. They must have known. How could they not?

There was no doubt in his mind they were coming for him. They would find him. At some point. They would come at night.

And when they did . . . he would go to jail.

* * *

Earlier that summer, my brother Ben and I, along with several other cousins, spent a week at my grandmother's farm in southern Minnesota.

Grandma regularly had several grandchildren on her farm throughout the summer. That particular week, there were about eight of us as well as a couple of aunts to cook for us, organize us, keep us clean, and generally herd us.

We loved our time on Grandma's farm. We played in the barns, ran through the woods, and built tree houses from old lumber in the shed. She got some good work out of us, too, as we picked berries, cut the grass, and entertained the younger cousins. On a really good day, she would let us drive the tractor.

Ben and I were the oldest. Naturally, we were seen as the more responsible cousins. As responsible as you can be when you're eleven and nine.

One morning, Grandma had the group out doing yard work. Ben and I were sent up to the house to get something from the basement. I don't remember what. But we obliged.

In Grandma's basement, there was an old wood stove; a toilet and shower; a laundry room; and a fruit cellar, where she kept homemade wine. In the hallway to the stairs, there was a rotary-dial landline telephone. You know, the almond-colored one. With the twenty-four-foot curly cord. They probably have them in museums now.

Again, what we'd been sent there to retrieve, I cannot recall. But I do remember one thing: we decided to make some phone calls.

Harmlessly, we dialed a few numbers, talked to some operators, reached some personal residences. In the process, we discovered—inevitably, organically, innocently—what it meant to make a prank call.

It made us laugh a little bit. So we dialed a few more numbers. Tried to call "Uncle Rolf." Laughed some more.

And then we got a good scolding from the operator.

We abruptly quit.

After a few minutes, we made it back out to the yard to finish chores with the rest of our cousins. We acted as if nothing had happened. I remember feeling a little bit guilty.

Just a little.

Deep inside.

Later that afternoon, we spotted a car coming up the long gravel drive. It was a county deputy vehicle. Grandma and the aunts went over to talk with the deputy while we cousins continued our chores. Eventually, we replaced yard work with a Frisbee game.

After a few minutes, the adults—the deputy included—came over to where we were playing.

Uh-oh.

The deputy asked if any of us had made some phone calls earlier that day.

Ben and I glanced at each other quickly but then played dumb.

"No, sir. We didn't make any phone calls."

At the time, I imagined we were very convincing. Looking back now, from a seasoned parent's perspective, I know so much more.

The deputy—well-meaning, I suppose—lectured all of us about how important it is not to play with phones. He told us prank calls come with large consequences—including up to ninety days in jail.

Ninety days in jail . . .

Those words instantly haunted me. I was certain I was bound for jail. And not just overnight. For NINETY DAMN DAYS!

I didn't know how my brother felt, but I was scared shitless. Maybe because I was the oldest and I felt I was supposed to be the responsible one.

Or maybe because I was eleven. A portion of my young brain knew, on some conscious level, that my fear was irrational. Unjustified. But only a small portion. The majority of my young mind was convinced that an officer would actually throw an eleven-year-old into jail for ninety days.

Fear emerges from the irrational.

I went to bed that night terrified. The next night, terrified.

The entire week at Grandma's house, I couldn't stop thinking about the consequences. Ninety days in jail. I felt guilty. I felt fear. It ate at me. I had trouble eating. Trouble sleeping. I couldn't let it go.

I decided never to tell anyone. Ever. I told myself that I just needed to get back home. Then I could relax, and my fear would go away.

I returned home.

The fear didn't go away.

So, every night, I wrapped the sheet and blanket snug over my head and around my body, leaving only my face peeking out, with my back to the windows, and kept the shades drawn shut. I lay on my right side, with my head tilted toward the door, away from the windows. I was certain the police were coming to get me.

I slept that way for over a year. Maybe more. I don't remember when the fear really went away, but it eventually did.

Fear permeates boundaries.

But even when I was a teenager, I'd remember those sleepless nights. I'd still wonder, even if briefly, *Are the police still looking for me . . . ?*

I never spoke about my fear. I never mentioned a word about it until I was in my midtwenties. And even then, I only shared it as a laughable story with friends.

By that point in my life, I was no longer afraid of the police coming in the middle of the night. Instead, I was afraid that maybe Grandma remembered that event, and that maybe she'd thought poorly of me all those years. In other words, an eleven-year-old's fear of going to jail had morphed into a twenty-five-year-old's fear of being a disappointment to his grandma.

Fear compounds itself.

Today, almost forty years later, I can say that the fear associated with this event is entirely extinguished. I'm of course no longer afraid the police are coming to get me. And I am no longer afraid that my grandmother might think poorly of me. I prefer the windows—and even shades—open at night. I loathe blankets too tightly wrapped around me.

But I still sleep on my right side.

Fear creates habits.

***

That's a cute story, Gerd, you say. *But I'm an adult. What does this have to do with me?*

I know. I know you're an adult. I know you aren't making prank calls anymore. I hope not, at least. And even if you are, I know you aren't concerned about going to jail for it.

I also know that you're much smarter, much more capable, and much healthier than eleven-year-old Gerd. And I know that the things you fear today are different from the things eleven-year-old Gerd feared.

I know.

One hundred percent.

Except . . . I know that your brain, today, deals with fear the same way eleven-year-old Gerd's brain did then. Then or now, you or me—it's all the same. Fear has the same functions, same brain processes.

Fear affects us in miraculous and unpredictable ways. It causes anxiety. It bears persistent, irrational thoughts. It affects our long-term behaviors. It alters our lives.

FEAR CREATES HABITS.

Fear emerges from irrational thoughts.

Fear permeates boundaries.

Fear compounds itself.

Fear creates habits.

That day on Grandma's farm will forever be imprinted in my memory. But what's most fascinating about fear is that sometimes we can't trace its origin to a seminal event.

Sometimes it just creeps in silently . . . like weeds in the garden.

Poor Man's Mustard

As early as the 1850s, settlers from Europe and Asia introduced garlic mustard to the United States. This easy-to-grow plant was used for cooking and medicinal purposes. It was easy to grow. It smelled like garlic. It helped control erosion. It was easy to grow.

Did I mention it was easy to grow?

In fact, it was so easy to grow that it became known as poor man's mustard because anyone could get their hands on it. (Because . . . it was easy to grow.)

Poor man's mustard takes two years from germination to full seed production. It begins small, and it's hard to identify. Then it grows. Quickly.

Eventually, poor man's mustard has the power to take over an entire area, creating a dense underbrush on forest floors. It absorbs light, water, and soil nutrients, preventing other plants from sprouting.

Not to mention, poor man's mustard releases chemicals into the soil that hinder the growth of other plant species. This means it's allelopathic. From Greek origin, *alleo* means "mutual," and *pathos* means "suffering." Poor man's mustard, by nature, makes other plants suffer.

Settlers had good intentions when they brought this plant to the United States. It was meant to have both savory and medicinal benefits. Instead, it obliterates biodiversity. It chokes out other plant life. It weakens the entire ecosystem. It destroys opportunities.

Poor man's mustard acts in the forest like fear acts in your brain. Fear grows easily, beginning as a small seed of irrational uncertainty. In that germination stage, it can be hard to identify.

But then, seemingly suddenly, it overtakes everything. It weakens the ecosystem of your life. It destroys your opportunities. It creates suffering.

FEAR DESTROYS YOUR OPPORTUNITIES.

The enemy to profound space—and to many other problems—is fear.

Dealing with poor man's mustard is not an easy task. Once it's established, you can't really "control" it at all. The only option is to remove it entirely—to manually pull it by its roots. It's a painstaking affair.

Dealing with fear is similar. It takes effort. It involves digging deep and getting below the surface, down to the roots. It involves discovering new disciplines to replace the habits your fear developed. It involves getting beyond preambles, making decisions to be courageous, and discovering your profound space. It's hard work.

But once you tackle your fear, your opportunities will flourish, not suffer. Your goals will become clearer, cleaner, closer, and more attainable, tangible, palpable. To call back to the earlier story about me out on the Kinnickinnic River, you will catch fish . . . and discover yourself along the way. You will become great at managing your emotions.

You will resolve the mystery of courage.

We all have fears—big, small, justified, irrational. Having fears does not mean you are weak. It means you are normal. Totally and completely normal.

But if you hold on to those fears, they will grow slowly, silently, over the years. They will overtake you. They will only make your opportunities suffer.

So rather than continuing to suffer, why not face your fear head on? Begin to identify what frightens you. Name it. Describe it. Pull it up by its roots. Take ownership of it. That is how you learn to cope with and prevent fear. That is the initial work of courage.

The next step of courage is the real key. You must *act*.

An action involves a decision. When faced with fear, you always have a decision to make: you can ignore it, or you can address it.

Courage addresses fear with action. This is what makes courage one of the most universally honored societal character traits. It is the growth-minded decision in response to fear.

And to vulnerability.

Cautiously Curious: The Case for Vulnerability

As a consultant, I occasionally get asked about my thoughts on failure. I don't mean the type of failure that leads to learning and growth. I mean real, honest failure that leads to an unfulfilled life.

Increasingly, my response goes something like this: *If you want to see true failure, then look for someone who refuses to acknowledge vulnerability or who doesn't take it seriously.*

That's a loaded word, isn't it? *Vulnerability.*

But we would be remiss to delve this deep into the topic of fear without addressing the importance of vulnerability.

Courage wouldn't exist without vulnerability. In fact, emotional vulnerability is necessary if you want to create profound space. Exponential growth begins with your willingness to be emotionally vulnerable.

Fear and vulnerability are inextricably linked on the way to creating your profound space. As you might guess, vulnerability is a close cousin of fear. But vulnerability is a little different. A little more nuanced.

Fear is an innate fight-or-flight response to a real or perceived threat. If fear were a person, she would say, "No way! I'm not doing *that*!" Her immediate response would be to turn away and avoid any perceptible threat or to fight the threat immediately.

Fear is perhaps the most powerful human emotion. Fear can cause stress, bring forth anger, produce depression, and influence your daily (even hourly) decisions. It can mold and shape you more powerfully than any other emotion.

But vulnerability can mediate that fear, even coax it into courageous action.

If vulnerability were a person, she would say, "This seems risky. This makes me nervous. But I'm gonna check it out anyway." She would be cautiously curious. She would be aware of her emotional reaction to the potential threat, but she would resist disengaging. She wouldn't let her fear determine the outcome.

This is how vulnerability acts like a mediator. It's the go-between that allows you to remain emotionally engaged. Cautious but curious. Which, in turn, allows you to make cognitive and rational decisions rather than emotional and reactive decisions driven by fear.

In other words, vulnerability gives you opportunities to get past fear and move toward success. In contrast, fear reacts to situations, often taking away opportunities, limiting you to fight-or-flight.

This all sounds great on paper, right? The hard part is, vulnerability is uncomfortable. Many of us greatly prefer not to feel vulnerable. Even though vulnerability is simply a part of life in both small and big ways, we refuse to acknowledge or recognize it.

VULNERABILITY ACTS LIKE A MEDIATOR. VULNERABILITY GIVES YOU OPPORTUNITIES TO GET PAST FEAR AND MOVE TOWARDS SUCCEED.

But despite the discomfort, vulnerability is a deeply powerful position. When you expose yourself to vulnerability, you are at the precipice of something important. That's why I call these *precipice moments.*

Precipice moments are profound space. Precipice moments change your life. Precipice moments are opportunities to be courageous. (In the next section you will read about ACME Design. See if you can recognize the precipice moment in their business.)

Having courage means having the willingness and strength to be vulnerable and to respond accordingly. That is what happens when you engage in profound space.

And the results are exponential.

You cannot be courageous without some degree of vulnerability. In fact, without vulnerability, you don't need courage to act. You just simply . . . act. Therefore, being vulnerable is actually a prerequisite to being courageous.

So instead of resisting vulnerability, we should *seek* it out. If you want to get stronger in courage, learn how to flex your vulnerability muscle.

Feel anxious after a disagreement in the workplace? Flex your vulnerability. Feel excited about a new project yet also stressed because you have a lot of work ahead? Flex your vulnerability. Feel hurt by something your spouse said? Flex vulnerability.

The better you are at recognizing and embracing your vulnerability, the more opportunities you'll have to act with courage. The better you are at distinguishing between fear and vulnerability, the more opportunities you'll have to keep that poor man's mustard from growing inside you, causing you to suffer.

Remember what I said above about vulnerability and failure? Do you get it now?

If you want to see failure, look for someone who refuses to feel vulnerable. You will see lackluster performance, artificial confidence, and disingenuous behavior. Ultimately, you will see someone allowing fear to take the lead role in a melodrama of avoidance.

That's failure. The refusal to grow by avoiding vulnerability.

On the other hand, the ability to leverage vulnerability for courageous action is among the chief human characteristics to fulfillment and achievement. When you take action, even when vulnerable and afraid, you will progress.

That's success. That's profound space. That's the mystery of courage.

For this reason, courage revolves around one decision. The decision to *act*.

The Resolution: Action

"Action is the foundational key to all success." This wisdom, often attributed to Pablo Picasso, seems reasonable, if not simplistic. Obviously, you have to *do something* in order to *achieve something*.

Yet this wisdom is multiplied when it comes to solving the mystery of courage. Action is, indeed, the momentum of courage and therefore a key to success. There are those who *say* they are going to do something, and those who *actually do* what they say. Action is what differentiates the courageous from the cowardly.

ACTION IS WHAT DIFFERENTIATES THE COURAGEOUS FROM THE COWARDLY.

Remember, most fear is contrived by your own mind. Most of it is irrational and emotionally charged. Vulnerability neutralizes fear through the power of cognitive wherewithal and emotional regulation. Action gives you aim, direction, and clarity. Action gives you movement and momentum.

If you're paralyzed in the shadow of fear, take action. *Any* action.

A No-Action Action?

In 2016, I consulted for a small organization we'll call ACME Design. They had roughly eighty employees. Nine key leaders, including the owner, served as decision-makers.

The leaders were very high achievers. They were motivated, decisive, and direct. And as a group, they typically aligned when it came to big decisions for the company.

For two decades, they'd led ACME to one success after another. In their niche market, there were no other players. That meant they enjoyed the relative comfort that comes with easy sales, increasing revenues, and no competition.

But then a new start-up appeared on the scene. Even though this company was less established, it made headway in the market, thanks to its drive and flexibility to offer competitive rates.

Suddenly, ACME was facing competition. Stiff competition.

This new development set ACME back on its heels. The leaders needed to act in response to this competition, but they couldn't agree on how. They were at a stalemate, locked in conflict over three options.

One option was to stay the course, offering their same services and rates and relying on the same relationships they'd built over time. "This would remind our customers why they chose ACME in the first place," one leader explained. The approach would especially work if the start-up happened to make a mistake or if it were forced to raise their initial rates, which ACME had deemed unsustainable for such a fledgling company.

Another option was for ACME to overhaul its products, revamp its services, and put a new face on the company. The sentiment behind this was "This would show the marketplace that we have expertise *and* fresh ideas."

Yet another option was for ACME to seek to buy out the new company. "This would ensure that ACME would remain the dominant force—the only force—in the market," one of the leaders reasoned.

The leadership group dedicated several meetings to these three ideas. They created spreadsheets and polarization charts. They listed pros and cons. They leveraged feasibility exercises. They generated mock plans with potential outcomes and expectations.

By the time I met with them, they'd spent fifteen weeks in this mire.

In our first meeting, I asked the leaders to summarize their situation. "Our team is firmly split about which direction ACME should go," the CEO said. "Our leadership is frustrated and can't agree."

Naturally, I was curious about this "firm split." Probing deeper, I asked each of the leaders a simple question: "Which option seems the most reasonable, effective, and necessary to *you*?"

One by one, they all hedged. No one had a definitive answer. That is, no one was willing to *admit* a definitive answer.

Each leader wanted the perfect plan for ACME's future. They each wanted an absolute guarantee of success. But none of the three options could deliver such a guarantee. Each option had its own set of pros and cons and risks and benefits—as all those spreadsheets, charts, and exercises had revealed.

I see this a lot with high achievers. The pressure to make the "right" decision is often an overwhelming battle between overthinking and overfeeling. And if not overwhelming, then at least extremely inefficient.

The leaders at ACME Design were very familiar with ease, success, and consensus. They were *not* familiar with challenge, failure, and disagreement. They were familiar with momentum, not with stagnation. The company was hanging in the balance, waiting for their decision. But they were paralyzed.

As we worked together, we realized we'd discovered something much more powerful than a "firm split." We'd discovered fear. And more importantly, a lack of courage to face it.

Courage is not about being right. Rather, it's about taking action even at the risk of being wrong. It's about establishing momentum.

Courage is grounded in two qualities: determination and decision. The determination to face a challenge, and the decision to act in the face of fear.

Remember Captain Rostron? Answering the *Titanic*'s call for aid required determination and decisiveness. There were no guarantees, only plenty of risks. But he still took action.

So how could the ACME leadership team go from wavering and conflicted to determined and decisive? They needed to take momentous action.

But most immediately, they needed to muster up some courage.

Courage must be built on something other than the expectation of perfect success. It must be based on values and vision. (We will discuss values and vision more thoroughly in the autonomy section.) It must be based on who you are and how you define yourself—identity.

For two decades, ACME Design had been the only player in their niche, with no competition and very little experience with failure. Being the "only one" was engrained not only in their identity but also in their measure of success.

But now they were standing face-to-face with a competitor. More importantly, they were standing face-to-face with the reality that their definition of identity (and success) was suddenly obsolete. Regardless of which option they chose, it meant they needed to create a new identity and a new future for themselves. They needed to see themselves anew.

In a brief session, we delineated ACME's company values. We revisited their collective vision for ACME and its partners for the future.

With the values and the vision as the baseline for decision-making, we then gave the three options a fresh look. We made three columns on the whiteboard in the conference room, and we listed the benefits and the drawbacks of each potential decision.

And then, I offered a fourth option that needed to be entertained: AMCE Design could make no decision.

When I added this as a fourth column on the whiteboard, I received a few chuckles.

But this was no joke. Choosing to make no decision *is* a decision. It's the decision to remain paralyzed. To dwell in fear.

So I forced the leaders to list the benefits and the drawbacks of this fourth option. I had to work hard to keep them focused and serious. I didn't let them off the hook. At the end, everyone realized this option had the longest list of drawbacks.

CHOOSING TO MAKE NO DECISION *IS* A DECISION. IT'S THE DECISION TO REMAIN PARALYZED. TO DWELL IN FEAR.

At this point, I turned to the leaders of ACME Design. "Do you feel better or worse about your decision?" I asked.

"Do you mean better or worse about our *options*?" one of them clarified.

"No," I said pointedly. "Fifteen weeks ago, when you began this conversation, each of you made the decision to make no decision. Each of you chose to avoid the risk of being wrong. Do you feel better or worse about it now?"

With that, this leadership group suddenly realized that their fear had already come true: by making no decision, they had already made the *wrong* decision.

By the end of the session, the leaders made a *new* decision and chose a direction. A direction based on their values and their vision.

I'm sure you're dying to know which option they chose. But it doesn't matter. Not for our purposes here.

What matters is that the ACME leaders finally realized that their lack of courage was contributing to the problem. They realized they had wasted valuable time. They realized that all three options had potential benefits as well as potential risks—but that the risks were tangible enough to manage and navigate. And they had the determination to move forward because they trusted the vision.

They also realized that the fourth option—the no-decision decision—was the greatest risk of all. Most importantly, they realized that failing, even accidentally, can ultimately lead to making new, better decisions. They realized that failure was a better alternative than making the no-decision decision.

Again, courage is not about being right or seeking perfection or securing guarantees. It's about seeing through the illusion of confidence. It's about providing momentum in an otherwise stagnant situation. It's about facing the challenge of fear. It's about resolving that challenge with action.

This is the mystery of courage. When you choose to enter into this mystery, you choose to enter profound space. Here's how.

Choose Courage

As the story goes, hip-hop artist Nas once reached out to music legend Prince about collaborating on a song.

"Do you own your masters?" Prince asked.

The simple question caught Nas by surprise. "I don't," he admitted. "And I'm far from it."

"When you own your masters," Prince replied, "give me a ring."

When a musical artist produces a song, there is a master recording. All subsequent recordings are taken from this master to maintain purity, quality, and uniformity.

Not many artists own the masters of their own songs.

When a musician signs with a music label, the contract typically grants ownership of the master recordings to the label (or the producer). Whoever owns the masters has the legal power to license those songs or that album as they wish, and they will receive royalties in return.

This means that most artists give up ownership of their own artistry.

Prince understood all this. Nas wasn't the only one to hear his wisdom. Prince also shared it with the world in a 1986 *Rolling Stone* interview: "If you don't own your masters, your master owns you."

"IF YOU DON'T OWN YOUR MASTERS," PRINCE SAID, "YOUR MASTER OWNS YOU."

You can imagine, then, what it means for artists to own their masters in the music business. It is an extremely profitable position. A powerful position.

Owning your masters in life is likewise very powerful.

Fear is a master.

Rev. Dr. Patrick Keifert once said, "That which you fear is your god. What you fear—it lords over you."

Think about your fears. Even just the seemingly simple ones. Fear of embarrassment. Fear of missing out. Fear of failing. Fear of looking foolish. Fear of judgment. Fear of asking or saying or doing the wrong thing.

But these simple, small, little fears generate power. Soon, they balloon into prevailing thoughts, obstructive feelings, incessant flooding of pain or trauma, and anger you refuse to confront. Small fears can compound the prevalence of substance abuse, drive debilitating perfectionism, and add undue complexity in your relationships. Small fears can cause stagnation.

When you allow even "simple" fear to command and direct your actions, you allow it to lord over you and your life. You allow it to enslave your soul.

You allow it to become your master.

Ultimately, you are responsible for the decisions, thoughts, ideas, emotions, attitudes, and expressions that govern your life. But taking responsibility is one thing; taking ownership is another.

So I ask the question: Do you own your masters, or do your masters own you?

You *can* own your masters. How?

By choosing courage.

By seeing through the illusion of confidence.

By facing the challenge of fear.

By resolving that challenge through action.

Choose courage, and you own your masters. You will begin to create profound space in your life.

I promise.

But then more will be required of you.

When it comes to creating profound space, courage alone is not enough. Yes, courage gets you going, gets you learning, gets you owning your fears and your life.

But then what do you do with everything you learn?

This is when we enter the mystery of insight.

Resolving the Mystery of Insight

WE ARE CREATING profound space. We have resolved the mystery of courage, the replacement for waiting around for confidence. As we continue creating profound space, we must now resolve the mystery of insight. And just like the mystery of courage, insight bears three components: an illusion, a challenge, and a resolution.

As we learned in the previous section, developing courage is deeply tied to controlling your emotions. From here, we are going to take a turn and focus less on emotions and more on your cognitions.

In this section we'll cover how insight is confused with the illusion of knowledge. We'll illustrate how knowledge doesn't help you unless you know what you *do* with that knowledge. Namely, that you undergo a transformation.

So let's resolve the mystery of insight.

a. The Illusion: Knowledge
b. The Challenge: Wilderness
c. The Resolution: Curiosity

The Illusion: Knowledge

The irony of knowledge is that the more you know, the more painfully aware you become of how little you know.

It's true.

In fact, I believe that how much you know rarely matters at all, especially if your knowledge serves no purpose. On the other hand, if you use your knowledge to grow and change how you impact the world around you—well, then, you have generated insight. And insight is powerful.

To put it another way, it's one thing to simply realize that olives are fruit. That's *knowledge*. It's another thing to know not to put that kind of "fruit" in my fruit salad. That's *insight*.

KNOWLEDGE IS TRIVIAL. INSIGHT IS TRANSFORMATIONAL.

Knowledge is trivial. Insight is transformational.

That leaves us with this: you may gather knowledge inside your head yet learn very little. That's trivial. Or you can be transformed by that knowledge.

That's insight.

Sounds easy.

It's not.

From Transistor to Transformation

Insight indicates learning. And learning indicates that change has occurred. You cannot learn without being changed.

With the invention of the first transistor in 1947, the world was changed forever. Transistors regulate and amplify electrical signals, acting as switch gates for flowing current. This technology allowed for the development of such products as pocket calculators, pacemakers, hearing aids, cameras, and, of course, the personal computer.

Transistors were perhaps the most influential invention of the Industrial Revolution. So influential, in fact, that they ended the Industrial Revolution altogether.

INSIGHT INDICATES LEARNING. AND LEARNING INDICATES THAT CHANGE HAS OCCURRED. YOU CANNOT LEARN WITHOUT BEING CHANGED.

The central concept of the Industrial Revolution was, of course, industry. That is, the economy relied heavily on *making* things. Ironically, *making* the transistor caused the Western economy to move from making things to *knowing* things. This shifted the world from the Industrial Revolution to the Information Age.

Because of the transistor, the world was transformed. Some companies had the insight to transform with it.

Others did not.

Take Encyclopedia Britannica, for example. For over two hundred years, Encyclopedia Britannica printed the world's information in books. They dominated the information subscription market. Many homes worldwide had two bookshelves in their living room or den dedicated to a set of *Encyclopedia Britannica*.

But the Information Age changed everything, thanks to the rise of computer technology and the ability to store mass amounts of information in small spaces. In 1993, Microsoft launched Encarta, a CD-ROM encyclopedia. Within three years, Encyclopedia Britannica's sales dipped by half.

Why?

Even though Encyclopedia Britannica sold information, their company culture and business model centered around printing. They understood themselves as a printing company, not an information company. They valued their printing tradition. They valued what they already knew (or believed they knew). They valued the stability that had gotten them ahead over the centuries.

So when Encarta showed up, Encyclopedia Britannica scoffed at the digital delivery model. They didn't have the insight to see that Encarta was, truly, an information company and that they were just new enough and agile enough to do whatever it took to deliver that information.

Encyclopedia Britannica nearly didn't survive. In fact, they wouldn't have survived had they not learned to change. They learned to deliver information with the latest technology, and they finally halted their hardcover volumes in 2012. Their survival required them to change the way they understood themselves: from a printing company to an information company.

Although Encyclopedia Britannica never returned to become the dominant force they once enjoyed, they are still alive today, in digital form. And that's only because they finally recognized that they needed to break old patterns of thinking. They had to let go of what they *knew* best: printing encyclopedia sets. They had to embrace the next era of information delivery.

They had to become insightful.

Insight indicates learning. And learning indicates change.

If Encyclopedia Britannica hadn't begun to value insight, they may have ended up like Kodak.

Remember Kodak? (Or for some of you, have you ever heard of Kodak?)

Kodak was a camera and film manufacturer. You paid for their camera. You paid for their film. You paid, repeatedly, for them to develop your photos. It was a brilliant business model. (Much like today's model of razor companies selling blades. You always need another blade.)

But then the Information Age ushered in digital photography. Ironically, Kodak had invented the first digital camera, back in 1975, but they didn't fully incorporate it into their business plan. They stuck with film cameras and film developing.

Other competitors developed digital cameras and envisioned a future where handheld digital cameras were commonplace. Companies like Canon, Fujifilm, and Sony were major players. Meanwhile, Kodak stuck to business as usual, selling and developing your film. They believed there was no valid alternative to a printed picture.

When digital cameras became mainstream, Kodak's market share crashed, as fewer and fewer people needed film and developing. In an attempt to hedge their losses, Kodak developed a digital camera with a docking station for at-home printing.

Then in 2001, Kodak acquired Ofoto, a website that allowed users to upload their photos and share them with friends and family. Sounds like an early form of social media, right? (Remember, Facebook wouldn't come along until 2003.)

Kodak could have grown Ofoto into an innovative new idea, like an online photo storage. Instead, they used it as another attempt to drive customers back to photo printing. A failed attempt. They used a new idea to keep an old business model alive. They knew photo printing, and they wanted to stick with what they *knew*. It was like trying to convince a river to change course.

In 2012, Kodak filed for bankruptcy.

Kodak's knowledge didn't help them. They knew photo printing, yes. What they failed to realize was that they were never in the photo-printing business in the first place. They didn't have the insight to realize that they were actually in the memory-sharing business—and that memories were much easier to store and organize in digital format.

If they'd understood they were in the memory-sharing business—an evergreen business—they would have made different decisions. Instead, they did everything they could to convince the world it needed to continue developing and printing photos.

We are told we need knowledge—more and more knowledge—to succeed. We are told "Stick to what you know" and "The more you know, the higher you will go."

Those are partial truths. Illusion.

We need insight—knowledge that creates change.

Insight indicates learning. And learning indicates change.

This is as true for individuals as it is for corporations.

Your Personal Business

Do you know what business you're in? I don't mean your professional business. I mean your personal business.

For instance, let's say your goal is to lose twenty pounds. So you might see yourself in the dieting business, the running business, the weightlifting business, the fasting business, or the calorie-counting business. You can view this in a lot of ways, depending on your tactics for losing weight.

But the thing about tactics (what you do and know) is that they can easily morph into identity (who you are). They begin to define us. Soon, you see yourself as a *dieter,* not just as someone who is dieting. You lose sight of the end goal.

But what happens to your identity when your tactics don't produce the results you want? That is, what happens when you *know* walking and *identify* as a walker, yet you can't walk off those last eight pounds? (Like how Kodak *knew* film development yet couldn't convince the world to keep developing photos.)

It's easy to think you need to double down. To recommit to the tactic. If you've been walking twenty thousand steps a day to no avail, then you might bump it up to thirty thousand. The more your sense of self is wrapped up in this tactic—in this "business model"—the more you'll stick with it, even if you're not seeing results.

As you can probably guess by now, this is where insight is necessary. Insight helps you change the tactics to accomplish your desired result. It's about being changed by what you are learning. The key is to know what business you are *truly* in.

As we recall, Encyclopedia Britannica eventually figured out it needed to be in the information business, not the book-printing business. As we also recall, Kodak never figured out it should have been in the memory-sharing business, not the photo-printing business.

So, remember those twenty pounds you're trying to walk off?

You might be in the wrong business.

Your challenge is to use your insight to discover your *true* goal, from a broader perspective. Which means your mindset must change. It's not about walking a certain number of steps, following a certain diet, fasting for a certain number of hours,

YOUR CHALLENGE IS TO USE YOUR INSIGHT TO DISCOVER YOUR *TRUE* GOAL, FROM A BROADER PERSPECTIVE.

and so on. It's not about losing a certain number of pounds. It may not be about losing weight at all.

Maybe it's about *health*. In that case, you're in the getting-healthier business.

Or perhaps it's about looking and feeling better. And then you're in the looking-and-feeling-better business.

See how that opens a wider door to success? There are many ways to be healthy. Many ways to look and feel better. Which means, you have many tactics at your disposal. You can walk and fast and run—and do silly dances with your kids and cook more meals at home and meditate and more.

In contrast, there are only a few tactics to lose twenty pounds, and they can all be fairly difficult—some even dangerous. Especially if you allow the tactics to drive your identity, rather than the other way around.

We will discuss identity in more detail in the Autonomy section. For now, the point is this: know what personal business you are in. If you want to grow, learn to transform your tactics. Learn to change what you *do*. And to connect what you *do* to *who you are*.

Insight creates a tactical transformation. It is a milestone toward success.

And transformation may ultimately be the distinction between your success and failure.

This is exactly what is required to create profound space.

Before you can solve the mystery of insight, you will face a special challenge. Look deep inside and come to grips with the fears, vulnerabilities, weaknesses, estrangements, habits, and mindsets that hold you back. Not only that, but also the dreams, visions, desires, and hopes that are grasping to come out.

Confronting these wild pieces and places will unlock amazing powers. Powers that I promise you will propel you toward a more fulfilling and accomplished life than you have ever known.

But you have to go there.

You have to confront the wilderness.

The Challenge: Wilderness

There I was. Naked. Alone. In the wilderness. My only companion, a patient wind, whispering her advice.

A loon surfaced quietly. With beads of water trickling off her feathers, she greeted me with a hallowing call, then departed into the depths.

Swirled with invigoration and intimidation—what was I doing? I was fatigued. Dehydrated. Nursing a bruised head and injured shoulder. Hunger was setting in. I had no food, and I was three days from my journey's end.

I was questioning everything I had set out to do. Yet somehow I was entirely *alive*.

This is the wilderness.

This is profound space.

It's time to confront this wilderness within.

Confront the Wilderness

The wilderness is a geography.
The wilderness is a psychology.

The wilderness is a geography. It's a physical place where natural order rules and human influence is subject. A place where you feel like a participant, a guest. Sometimes an uninvited one. A place where rain cleanses, sun scorches, lightning threatens, and wind exerts its unadulterated force. A place where fears and ingenuity unite and your vulnerability is rewarded with new understanding.

The wilderness is a psychology. A cognitive-emotive place where ambiguity and uncertainty rule. A place where uncontrollable forces put identity to the test. A place where fears are met with curiosity and deep desires emerge from behind your preambles. A place where you face realities you prefer not to be true and your vulnerability is rewarded with new insight.

You may never enter the geographic wilderness, deliberately subjugating yourself to an uncertain environment for the sake of growth and discovery. But entering the wilderness within yourself is no less a path to profound space. A path that will help you to grow, complete your spectacular vision, and take you on a journey all your own. You will visit places that are intimidating and exciting, simultaneously. Places that obligate you to name and face your fears and to seek responsibility.

Confronting your personal wilderness allows you to go from great to exponentially *more*.

Ready to take the first step?

Set aside your phone, your social media account, your email. Grab a blank notebook and a pencil or pen, and go off somewhere by yourself so you won't be distracted.

CONFRONTING YOUR PERSONAL WILDERNESS ALLOWS YOU TO GO FROM GREAT TO EXPONENTIALLY *MORE*.

Once you're set, take a minute to think about the things in your life that are problematic. Can you list them?

I don't mean to list all the things other people think you should change. Make sure it's your list and not somebody else's.

Forget other people's values. Forget what others expect of you, demand of you, or anticipate of you. Forget the vision someone else has for you in your life. Forget the "sins" the world and your family believe you've committed. Forget the things that are intended to make you feel shamed or less-than or to soothe someone else's ego. Set all that head-trash aside.

Instead, think deeply about the things *you* know, deep down in your heart of hearts, that hold you back. What are the actions or inactions that keep you from reaching the finish line? What are the things that you don't spend enough time doing or spend too much time doing that prevent you from being productive, successful, and fulfilled? What are *your* values? *Your* objectives and goals?

This exercise isn't that hard. In fact, I suggest it might even be easy. Probably too easy. It's so easy that you may already be thinking that it's gonna be boring.

Well, if it's so easy, go do it! Make your short list. I know you can come up with a few things.

And I know you can do this without getting distracted—or at least without getting entirely derailed. Do you notice how easily distractions can slip into your mind? Like, *I have to check that email,* or *I wonder what my friends are doing on social media.*

That's head-trash too, so forget it. Forget all the clutter that takes up space in your brain and in your life. Forget about all that trash that tries to prevent boredom or even relieve anxiety. Forget all that stuff.

Just continue to sit quietly with yourself, your notebook, your pencil, and nothing else.

Do you like the position you're in? Do you like who you are as a person? What do you love about yourself? What do you find despicable or prefer were different?

Where do you want to be in two years? Five years? Ten years? What kind of a person do you want to be? What do you want to be doing for work? In your personal life? With whom do you want to be hanging around?

Where do you find meaning in your life right now? Or how about in five years or ten years? Are you fulfilled? Are you unfulfilled? Is there anything you could be doing to propel yourself into a life of meaning and fulfillment?

What are you doing (or not doing) that is damaging your trajectory? What are you doing that is holding you back? What demons do you face or fears do you hold on to? What addictions do you have?

No one is reading this. Be honest with yourself.

You can do this. You can make this happen. You can confront your wilderness.

Remember—you're just making a list. You do not need to solve any of these issues right now. All you have to do is become aware of your wilderness.

Write down the things that are important to you and the things that you know, deep down, need to change. Go into your profound space and own it. Go and spend quality time with the most important person in your life—*you*.

Are you doing it? Are you ready to set the book aside and go find some paper and a pen? Are you ready to engage in a responsible act that begins to create profound space?

Or are you planning to skip the exercise and move on to the next chapter?

Either way, what does your decision tell you about yourself?

Confront your wilderness.

Midway

Shouts came from down the street. Yelling. Screaming. People arguing. Volume escalating. A man and a woman, shouting back and forth. The sounds were getting closer. Coming down the sidewalk.

I'd been enjoying a quiet evening in my backyard in the Hamline-Midway neighborhood of Saint Paul, Minnesota. It's an eclectic neighborhood. You might consider it to be a mix of middle-to-lower-middle-class families. Mostly single-family homes with clapboard siding, sprinkled with a mix of multifamily dwellings and apartment complexes, especially near the main avenues of University and Snelling. University Avenue, which runs parallel to Interstate 94, is an east-west thoroughfare connecting Minneapolis and Saint Paul.

For many years, the neighborhood had suffered from—what I considered—a confused identity. Its very name, Hamline-Midway, indicates it's near Hamline University. But more importantly, it indicates it's midway between the hearts of Minneapolis and Saint Paul.

Midway.

Between two somethings.

Neither here nor there.

Historically, University Avenue served as a corridor of business activity. Sizable auto dealerships as well as blue-collar businesses once dotted the avenue. But since the collapse of the auto industry and the boom of suburban dealerships, many of those buildings had sat empty.

Nowadays, Hamline-Midway is up-and-coming. It's starting to see its era of development. With the rise of the Green Line light-rail system, construction of a nearby soccer stadium, and a lower tax base compared to neighborhoods south of I-94, professional families began snatching up three-to-five-bedroom houses and calling Hamline-Midway home.

Along with this rise of activity came all forms of gentrification as well as a budding identity of true diversity.

So there I was that particular evening, sitting on my patio, enjoying a cool and comfortable summer dusk, when the yelling and arguing came down the street. I couldn't see; I could only hear. My backyard was elevated off the sidewalk with a four-foot retaining wall, and a six-foot privacy fence that kept peeping eyes at bay.

From my side of the fence, I could tell the woman was walking by briskly, yelling, asking to be left alone. Not just crying. Sobbing.

Behind her, about sixty or eighty feet, the man was pleading with her to come back. His pleas turned to demands. Then threats.

"*Leave me alone!*" the woman shouted.

That was the last I heard from her. For a while.

After a quiet half hour, I heard something in the alley behind our detached garage. Some shuffling around. Faint crying. It sounded as though someone was talking on the phone.

I ignored it. But it persisted.

By now, the sun had set. I was generally vigilant around our neighborhood, especially after dark. I thought I would check out what was going on in the alley before calling it an evening.

Crying and bleeding from a cut just above her left brow, a woman in her midthirties sat hunched up against my neighbors' garage door, whispering to someone on her phone.

I approached cautiously but came into the light.

Quickly, she hung up.

"Miss, are you OK?"

"I'm fine, yes."

"You don't look OK . . . Can I get you something?"

"No, no. I just need to be here where it's dark." She seemed to stiffen up just a bit.

"Are you hiding from something . . . ?"

"Yes. My boyfriend. But it will be OK."

"Miss, my name is Gerd. Why don't you come and hide in my backyard? It's super private, and it's safe. I'll get you some water and maybe a bandage."

She readily agreed. So readily, in fact, that I was taken aback. I anticipated greater hesitance.

What have I gotten myself into?

She seemed to feel safe in my backyard—relatively so, considering she was bloody, crying, and on a stranger's patio. But she felt safe enough to tell me her story.

Her name was Jessica. Jessica had a two-inch cut over her left brow. She'd fallen down a flight of stairs.

After her boyfriend had hit her in the stomach.

And pushed her toward that flight of stairs.

I listened to Jessica's story. Every painful detail. I tried not to wince. I tried not to judge. Just listened.

Jessica was not working. She and her adult daughter depended on the boyfriend for money, food, shelter.

This wasn't the first time she'd been beaten by this man. He'd hit her before.

Jessica said that each time it happened, he would apologize once his anger wore off. He knew it wasn't right. He genuinely felt guilty. He'd say he'd never do it again. He'd mean it.

And each time, Jessica would want it to be true. She'd genuinely believe him. She'd accept his apology, and they'd go on living life.

Frustration. Fear. Pain. Fear. Dependance. Fear. Rushes of adrenaline. More fear.

I gave Jessica some water and helped clean and bandage her wound. She was swelling around her eye. We put ice on it.

Gradually, Jessica's sobbing gave rise to calm. She was no longer breathing heavily, and she didn't have the look of fear in her eyes. She began talking articulately about her experience. She was certainly in a logical headspace.

That's when we started discussing options—places where she and her daughter could get away from this abusive situation.

Jessica was hesitantly open to alternatives. *Hesitantly,* I say. It took some counsel, some convincing, but she ultimately agreed to call a victims' assistance service so we could discuss options with them.

She was even a little excited about one possibility we discovered. We found a shelter. They had one opening. It wasn't close, but I was willing to get her and her daughter there.

She verbally agreed.

At nearly that same moment, we heard yelling down the street. "Jessica! Where are you? I'm sorry! Come home! Jessica!"

The boyfriend.

I watched as Jessica's eyes instantly plunged from possibility and hope to immediate threat and danger. In the snap of a finger. It was fear. Jessica was terrified.

I remember as though it were two minutes ago.

She started talking a mile a minute. "I have to go. I have to go home. He's waiting for me. I don't want him to get mad again. If I don't go home, he'll find me eventually. I have to go."

I tried to object. I tried to get her thinking about the possibilities again. But it was too late. Her brain had slipped back into fight-or-flight. Only this time, she was fleeing *toward* the danger.

"I have to go. I don't want him to find me here. I can't be here. He'll be really angry if he knows I told you. Please, don't say anything to him. Please."

I promised her I wouldn't say anything to her boyfriend, under one condition: that she promised to come back if this happened again. That she would knock on my door, front or back. Didn't matter. That she would hide here. That she would be welcomed here. That she would leave her situation and find shelter, somewhere.

After a quick, unintentional promise, Jessica was out the back gate.

I wanted to stop her. I knew I couldn't.

I wanted to report it to the police, but the victims' assistance service had advised against it. Not to mention, I didn't know where she lived, what her last name was, or if she really was "Jessica."

I thought about following her. But I knew that would cause more harm than good.

So I let her go. Out into the neighborhood.

Midway.

Neither here nor there.

Into her own wilderness.

* * *

For those on the outside, it would be easy to look at Jessica and ask, "Why don't you just leave him?" It would also be easy to blame and judge her, saying, "You're choosing to stay. You're doing this to yourself."

Those sentiments are unfair. From a purely theoretical perspective, yes—Jessica did indeed have the power to make different decisions. But we cannot possibly fathom the fear she experienced and how much control it exerted over her.

Jessica was trapped midway between a current life of abuse and a potential life of safety. One life involved wishing things were different, and the other life involved affecting change to make it different.

We all get trapped midway.

But for many victims of abusive and toxic relationships, the fear of being physically harmed is far less than the fear of abandonment, of loneliness, of failure, of humiliation, and of other kinds of suffering. Overcoming those fears is extremely challenging. Jessica—in that moment—may not have been ready. Or she may not have had the strength.

Obviously, Jessica's story is severe. Not everyone can relate to the power of fear in a violent relationship.

But I share her story because we, like her, are all trapped midway. We all feel the distance, the void, between who we are and who we want to become. Between what we have and what we want. Between where we are and where we want to be.

We all feel the fear that keeps us neither here nor there. For some of us, these fears keep us from leaving toxic relationships. For others, they keep us from staying (or getting) sober, setting boundaries, eating healthy, addressing tough issues with coworkers or loved ones, holding others accountable, defining goals, finishing what we want to finish, or starting what we hope to begin.

WE ALL FEEL THE DISTANCE, THE VOID, BETWEEN WHO WE ARE AND WHO WE WANT TO BECOME.

When we get caught midway, why don't we "just do something" about it? Why don't I just do something about it? Surely, my midway is not as fearful as Jessica's.

I don't know what happened to Jessica. I hope she found the power to make different decisions in her life, whether on her own or with the help of others.

I hope she found a way to confront her wilderness.

I hope you do too.

The Great Chasm

In 2005, I was invited to consult for a nonprofit company that had left its parent organization over an internal disagreement. They invited me in to coach them through a visioning process intended to build organizational unity and cast a new direction.

I welcomed the chance to work with this group. The leadership team was very accomplished, consisting of finance professionals, small business owners, educators, a CEO of a local company, an agency marketing director, and a banker. These were intelligent, capable people, and a joy to work with.

Even better, everyone on the leadership team had experience with third-party consultants, and two of them worked with professional coaches on a regular basis. I was excited because often the largest hurdle is getting a group to trust the process. All signs indicated they were in.

Or were they?

Once we dove in together, we discovered that the identity of this group was in its infancy. That's not uncommon with a new organization. They didn't understand themselves well as an independent entity, outside the parent organization. They couldn't clearly define who they were, what they stood for, or where they were going. They didn't understand their common values. In short, they didn't know who they were.

Even after some work together, each member of the group had a different understanding of how to define this new organization, what it should look like, in which direction it should move, and in which activities it should engage. The differences weren't small either. They were vast. So vast, in fact, that three members hinted that remaining with the parent organization would have been better than the new direction one team member now offered.

This group had common hopes but for different reasons. They wanted to grow, but they suffered from a confused identity.

Despite this, they all agreed on one thing: they knew what they were *not*.

So we started there.

As we continued working, we discovered that they had allowed fear to prevent them from defining themselves. The departure from their parent organization had caused severe and painful conflict. Now they feared conflict in their new organization. So they withheld opinions, danced around tough issues, and avoided making courageous assertions.

Their fear pitted them midway between two stories: the story of who they used to be and the story of who they wished to be.

As you now know, it's a universal story that plays out in different ways for different people. When in this midway existence, the distance between your current state and your desired state can feel like a great chasm. This chasm can especially feel real when your old identity is driven by or created by fear or some other master.

This chasm is simply part of your wilderness landscape. It's the normal, necessary chaos that exists when you're neither here nor there, neither your old self nor your new self.

Once you enter your wilderness and begin to change, you will be challenged by fear, insecurity, and vulnerability. It will confuse your desires. It will leave you with an incomplete and disoriented identity. But an identity in motion is transformation in progress.

This is when insight begins to take hold.

AN IDENTITY IN MOTION IS TRANSFORMATION IN PROGRESS.

This nonprofit organization wanted unity and direction, and that proved to be a bigger challenge than they first realized. But nothing builds unity and direction better than standing on the edge of the chasm together and seizing the opportunity to cast a collaborative vision.

And in our work together, this organization was able to do that. By leveraging courage, insight, and (of course) time, this group of intelligent people was able to set a direction and build the unity they desired. Because they were willing to do that hard work, they are a success story even today.

They looked into their chasm together, then decided to change.

Together.

Change

I know you were taught that people don't change. Can't change.

You were reared to believe that once you reach adulthood, or perhaps even earlier, you're basically set in stone. That your behaviors, your tendencies, your responses to any given stimuli—it's all cast.

You were taught to believe that you are incapable of growing or changing in any substantial way. And once you firmly believed in this inability, you were taught to simply *accept yourself.*

That seems to be the mantra for our era. If you accept yourself, you'll be happy and fulfilled.

How's that going for you?

I don't believe self-acceptance is life's goal. At least not for a large number of us.

On one hand, we all want to value ourselves and appreciate who we are as unique humans without feeling the pressure to mold into someone else's vision. That's acceptance. That's good.

But more often than not, "accept yourself" is just a cloak for resignation. Resignation to your limitations. Your failures. Your weaknesses. Your unfinished goals. It seemingly grants you permission to stop trying to improve, grow, and become. Because when things get too damn hard, falling back on "accept yourself" is better than admitting "I quit."

Sure, there is power in owning and embracing your failures, but is that where you should leave it? Is self-acceptance really your end goal? Is that what fulfills you?

It just leaves you grasping for more, right?

Don't let self-acceptance become self-resignation. We all know how it looks and sounds:

I always dreamed of writing a book, but I'm not disciplined enough to do it, so I guess I won't.

I wish I could have more friends, but people don't like my opinionated nature, so I guess it ain't happening.

I'd love to lose twenty pounds, but I'm supposed to accept myself, so I guess I'm fine being unhealthy, regardless of what the medical research tells us about obesity.

DON'T LET SELF-ACCEPTANCE BECOME SELF-RESIGNATION.

Once you accept yourself in this way, you lose motivation. You give up on your potential. You quit growing. You quit becoming. You resign your personal business.

"Accept yourself" has become synonymous with *I don't want to put in the effort to change.*

So you don't change. You don't even believe you *can* change.

I don't believe that's what humans are made for.

The laws of physics and the laws of human nature are somewhat consistent. An object at rest remains at rest. An object in motion remains in motion. Unless, of course, either object is acted upon by a different force.

Life is full of "forces" that act on us, causing us to move, or rest, if we let them. Motivation is a force that moves us. Peer pressure moves us—sometimes for good, and other times not so much. "Accept yourself" is a force that can stagnate your growth.

But did you know your own mindset is a force? Your beliefs?

You believe you can't change. But what if you chose to believe that you can?

What if you chose to change?

***

I know you've been taught that people don't change. Can't change.

I know because I was taught that too.

I grew up believing that *people don't change* was the rule of life. It didn't matter how long you lived or what you experienced—on some basic level, you would remain the same.

Of course, you might change your clothes, your hair, your personal style. You might change your friends, although not frequently. And not drastically.

For most of my life, I believed that who you are today is who you would remain for life. The joyful presence you carry now would always remain. The hurts you carry now would forever be there. The way you see yourself, whether desirable or otherwise, would remain stable. Your abilities and capacities could not be increased. It was all set in stone.

That's what I learned to believe.

I think it was supposed to be some kind of comfort, to trust that things will remain the same. That I could, in some fantastical way, rely on people to remain constant. Including myself.

Knowing that I would always be me, I could therefore learn how to be content with myself, how to celebrate my gifts, and how to accept the things I'd prefer not to be. After all, *that's just how I'm built.*

But what if you choose something different? What if you just can't accept yourself? Or won't? What if you want more? Believe you are more? What if who you are today isn't who you want to be tomorrow?

Do you just accept that?

What if you know that you are made for more? I don't mean *more* in a consumeristic way or even a psychological way like *I'm not enough. I need more.*

I mean, what if you want to be better? What if you want to become a better parent, spouse, psychologist, custodian, skateboarder, art collector, wine connoisseur? What if you just want to become a more complete person? What if you want to become healthier in both body and mind? What if you want to—and know you can—expand your capacity?

What if you want to—and know you can—change?

But people don't change, the voice says. You are encouraged to believe this because not changing is the easy way out. It's the easy way out for you and the rest of the world.

It's easier if we collectively assume that whatever your problems may be, you will never get over them, never grow beyond them. That's an ironic comfort, isn't it? If *you* never grow beyond your problems, then *we* don't have to grow beyond our problems either. It's like an unspoken social pact.

The collective *we* doesn't want you to grow. Because that would make the rest of us look bad. And what if you successfully grow, but we try and fail? That would make the rest of us look really bad. It's so much easier—for us all—if you don't change.

Misery loves company, as the adage goes.

Many still believe this drivel. Perhaps even you do. I know I did until a few years ago.

I changed my way of thinking.

You can too.

People don't change is a lie.

People change. Can change. Do change.

I've watched lifelong addicts get sober.

I watched a seventy-year-old learn to skateboard to fulfill a lifelong dream. A sixty-five-year-old change his deeply held political beliefs because he started to see the world differently. A business owner close her thriving company because she no longer believed in what she sold.

People change.

I've watched a ten-year-old relearn to talk and walk after major head trauma. I've watched timid people-managers transform into catalysts of professional development. I've watched selfish executives awaken to the practices of servant leadership.

People change.

I've been welcomed into the profound space of countless hospital rooms, crisis centers, homeless shelters, and dining rooms. In these sacred places, I've watched people transform before my very eyes.

People change.

In profound ways.

I've watched people expose themselves to the wilderness of the world and the wilderness of themselves. I watched, awe inspired, as their desire to grow into something more manifested seemingly out of nowhere.

People change.

And I've watched hundreds of people set intentions to become more consummate, more successful, more fulfilled human beings simply because they wanted to be *more*.

People change.

I've dedicated my life to helping people expand their capacity. Because I believe most people want to become more, different, better.

People change.

People *want* to change.

People *can* change.

Especially if they understand that change doesn't have to be hard.

Making Change *Not* Hard: A New Way

Change can be hard. It can be taxing emotionally, mentally, even physically. It is ambiguous and causes uncertainty. It's a wilderness, for sure. No wonder most people stand at the precipice of change but then turn back around.

You can make change *not* hard.

What if you had the insight to confront your wilderness? What if you had a map? At the very least, what if you were willing to use courageous action to test it out?

Wouldn't that make a difference? Wouldn't that assist in making change *not* hard?

Maybe. Maybe not. But remember what we learned about courage: it begins with action in the face of feeling vulnerable. And change can be extremely vulnerable when we don't know what to expect. But if we can lean on a few principles of change to help us understand what's about to happen. That alone might be enough to make change . . . not easy, but *not* hard.

Every person and every organization respond to change in a unique way, but we all go through three predictable phases: an ending of the old way, a time of disorientation, and a consolidation of the new way.

Every change begins with an ending. This seems backward, doesn't it? Well, not really.

Before you embrace something new, you must end your relationship with what is being replaced. When you begin a new job, you end your old job. When you start to eat healthy, you end your old eating habits. When you have your first child (a big change!), you end your childless way of life.

During the ending phase, you might find yourself focusing on the past. You might feel denial or anger or sadness or anxiety. You might not be ready to accept that your old way of being is gone or that something new must rise in its place. During this time, it's easy to cling to the status quo. But in order for change to occur, you ultimately must say goodbye to your status quo. After all, this is what change *is*.

I call the second phase disorientation. When you move into this phase, you are . . . well . . . disoriented. Things can feel chaotic. That's because you said goodbye to the old way but don't yet fully understand the new way yet.

For most of us, this phase is very uncomfortable. People generally dislike uncertainty. This is what people think about when they say things like "Change is hard." But if you can embrace this moment, you'll see it's a time to try new things. To experiment. To be creative, collaborative, and open.

The disorientation phase will eventually transition into the consolidation phase. This is when your new ideas become routine, slowly but certainly. There likely won't be one, single moment when you suddenly "change." Unlike a light switch that immediately changes the light in the room, you'll likely *transition* from ending to consolidation. From the old way to the new way.

In time, your direction becomes clearer, your focus on the future becomes realer, and your efforts become more intentional. Eventually, you'll recognize that the consolidation is complete and that you've successfully created and embraced your new way.

There is a Greek term for this change: *metanoia*. It means "to see in a new way." Metanoia is often translated as *repentance* and understood with the modern cloaked baggage that comes with that word. But more acutely, it represents change. To change your mind. To see yourself, and the world, in *a new way*.

To experience change is to see the world a new way. Metanoia.

Of course, there's lots more to unpack in regard to these three phases of transition. But for our purposes here, I want you to have at least this basic understanding of what you'll go through when you decide to make a change.

To say it simply: Learn to end well, learn to be calm in the chaos, and learn to consolidate the new thing—three tangible skills.

Change isn't easy, but it doesn't have to be hard . . . if you're prepared for the process. That is, if you understand that all change begins with an ending, you'll be better equipped to say goodbye to your old way of doing things. If you know you're going to experience some misdirection and chaos for a while—and that it's actually normal—you'll find it easier be courageous, creative, and curious during that time. You will also be able to tell yourself, "This is normal—I will get through this." And if you realize that consolidating your new beginning won't happen overnight, you'll be ready to pinpoint success when you finally establish your new way.

We're not just talking about "change" here. We're talking about growth. About creating profound space. Whether you're starting a new job or trying to become a better parent, these phases of transition will help you understand your experience and be reliable as you confront your wilderness.

And the key takeaway is this: disorientation is the most important phase for creating profound space and developing a lasting change. As we said, disorientation is the phase most people appreciate the least. It's uncomfortable. It's chaotic. It's uncertain. It's called "the disorientation phase" for a reason, and many people prefer to jump over it as quickly as possible.

But like it or not, the disorientation phase is absolutely paramount. It's akin to confronting the wilderness. You must confront it and experience it in order to come out on the other side with a lasting, successful new way. This applies to your organization, your team, and you.

In order to face the mystery of insight, you must face the challenge of confronting the wilderness and all its discomforts. But the good news is, there is a resolution that eases the discomfort and makes the chaos and uncertainty worth it.

That resolution is curiosity.

The Resolution: Curiosity

Especially in a world of instant gratification, it's easy to believe you "fix" yourself immediately and "solve" all your problems *right now*. But no. You don't have to know everything, finish everything, or change everything about yourself at a moment's notice.

You simply start by being curious. Curious about yourself. About your hopes and dreams. Your fears and desires. Your preambles and profound space.

To be honest, not many of us fully understand curiosity. In fact, we're often wary of it. As children, we're naturally curious, but we quickly learn to inhibit this inclination. Schools tend to teach "right" and "wrong," and curiosity gets squelched by the desire to be "right." Over the years, a closed mindset calcifies on a subconscious level. The self-talk that accompanies this mindset is more powerful than you may think.

Don't let your desire for *rightness* squelch your curiosity.

Start by being curious about curiosity.

Curiosity is the resolution that allows us to grow past the illusion of knowledge and traverse into our wilderness. To experience, to explore, to discover, to understand.

Curiosity will relieve the confusion we feel during disorientation. It will soften some of your fears and vulnerabilities. It gives you something to focus on when discomfort looms.

Curiosity will lead you to discover more about who you are and who you want to be.

Curiosity doesn't judge or grade or evaluate. It takes in, absorbs, listens.

Curiosity does not know; it strives to understand.

Curiosity drives insight. And insight indicates change.

The Honorable Duel

Do you know what distinguishes a true duel from a common scuffle? A duel was a sign of mutual respect among equals. It was wrought with honor, rules of engagement, and dignity.

To be challenged to a duel meant that the issuer received the opponent as an equal, even though an offense had seemingly occurred between them. It meant the challenger respected the opponent enough to settle the disagreement in a proper way. Otherwise, the challenger would have simply stabbed the opponent from behind or clubbed them with a lesser weapon. The duel is sort of a primitive form of conflict resolution.

The importance of honoring one's opponent is part of biblical tradition also. Many of us know the oft-quoted passage about turning the other cheek. The main character, Jesus, teaches listeners that if someone strikes their right cheek, they should offer their left cheek as well. This is typically interpreted as a message of pacifism, but a deeper look reveals more.

In a right-hand-dominant world, being struck on the right side of the face means being *backhanded,* not outright punched. In biblical times, a backhand was a deliberate act of not only aggression but condescension. It was reserved for subordinates. To be backhanded meant the aggressor saw the victim as inferior. It was a statement of inequality and an assertion of dominance.

So when Jesus taught his followers to respond to a backhand by offering their left cheek as well, it was a message of defiance and honor. The victim was to invite the aggressor to treat them as an equal.

Fight with honor, or don't fight at all.

Make it a proper duel.

Wrestling with your wilderness is a proper duel, worthy of honor and respect. So is contending with your profound space.

At the end of a traditional duel, there was a clear winner and a clear loser. Depending on the rules of engagement, this could mean battling to the death.

But dueling with matters of profound space is not about winning and losing. In these duels, you want to seek a different kind of victory: the victory of growth.

In order to explore this concept, let's play with the concepts of *duel* and *dual*.

A duel represents polarized contention of opposite viewpoints. That is, two people face off, each with differing positions. There is a colossal chasm between these two people and two beliefs. This is dualism.

Want to see how this works in simple, real-world terms? Think about a time when you were presented with something new—new information, new tech, new procedures, new foods, whatever. Very likely, you gravitated toward one of two polar responses. You were either an early adopter, quickly committing to the new thing, or you were a resistor, refusing what was new.

Adoption and resistance are polar opposites—dualistic perspectives in this duel of change.

The thing is, most people are naturally resistors. According to organizational psychologist Nick Tasler, roughly two in three people struggle when presented with a significant pivot in direction. Their natural response is to resist the new information or the change.

As a change leader, I observe this two-thirds daily. With most individuals and organizations, I witness an immediate resistance toward any newness.

If you do the math, then, you can see how this duel of dualism plays out in a group situation. Within an organization or team, this polar construct can become contentious when adopters and resistors get frustrated with one another. This duel impedes growth.

In my work, most people assume it's my job to turn resistors into adopters. On the contrary, it's my job to challenge *both* adopters and resistors to think differently about their approach.

The truth is, neither side of this duel is "right." Blind adoption is not a better approach than immediate resistance. Resistance closes the door to growth, and early adoption can lead you into quick mistakes that inhibit trust.

The problem is the duel itself—the polarized mindset that says you must choose from one of only two options and then fight for it with your life. Engaging in this type of thinking can prevent growth on a personal and organizational level.

So how do you "win" this duel? How do you achieve the victory of growth when faced with the duality of adoption versus resistance?

With curiosity, of course.

The reason curiosity is so powerful is twofold. First, it avoids the tension of the duel between adoption and resistance. And again, this applies to both individuals and groups. When you're curious, you don't have to waste energy deciding which camp to join. You don't have to commit blindly as an early adopter, nor do you have to immediately close yourself as a resistor. You don't have to defend your position or your belief. It saves you from the duel.

Second, curiosity is powerful because it opens you up to uncommitted insight. Curiosity opens the door and all your senses. It allows you to learn, inquire, absorb, and grow. Curiosity is not committed to right or wrong, left or right, up or down. It's committed to discovery. Curiosity holds two opposites in tension together.

CURIOSITY AVOIDS THE TENSION OF THE DUEL BETWEEN ADOPTION AND RESISTANCE . . . BECAUSE IT OPENS YOU UP TO UNCOMMITTED INSIGHT.

This is where you enter profound space and discover insight. You can be amazed—and possibly transformed—without having to commit to a duel.

Dualism and dueling put you at a risk—not of death but stagnation. Curiosity opens you to growth. This is the difference between those who grasp and those who grow, those who fall short and those who achieve.

Curiosity is powerful. It takes effort.

Curiosity holds two opposing things in tension together.

Simul

In March 2017, my youngest brother, Max, died suddenly in his sleep. He was thirty-five years old, living alone in Chicago. One day, he didn't show up for work. His coworkers found him dead in his apartment.

Max had a zest for life. His early years taught him grit, which served him well in various carpentry trades and in over-the-road trucking.

Charismatic and kind, Max touched the lives of countless people. He made friends throughout the country, meeting people as he traveled. He would talk to anybody. And if someone needed something, he would help. No questions asked. At Max's burial, his friends shared a story of Max giving up his bedroom for several months, sleeping in his garage, so that his roommate's young daughter could have her own room until her dad stabilized his life.

Max kept his profound space well guarded with preambles. It wasn't until his death that we discovered he'd had a seventeen-year-long relationship with addiction.

We knew very few details. We learned he'd been in an auto accident that he—and the people in the vehicle he struck—were fortunate to have survived. The accident sent him to addiction treatment. At the time of his death, he had been out of treatment for six months. His toxicology report was clean.

Just as curiosity holds two opposing things in tension together, Max embodied a *both-and* quality. He had grit . . .

and was tenderhearted. He was open . . . and elusive. He was fun to be around . . . and at times abrasive. He was highly intelligent . . . and at times made unintelligent decisions.

We all have this tension in us. And there is a name for it.

The Latin term *simul* embodies this notion of *both-and*. It simply means "at the same time." Simultaneously.

In simple terms, if you've ridden a roller coaster, then you've experienced simul. You've experienced two seemingly opposite feelings at the same time: fear and joy. It doesn't make rational sense to us that we would experience these two feelings together, but it happens all the time, and it is normal.

Max, like all of us, reflected simul in many ways. We all have constructs in our profound space that seem to be at odds yet need to be expressed simultaneously. That's often why we tuck these pieces away in a symbolic cigar box of profound space—because they don't make sense to us.

We tuck them away because we don't yet understand that these contentious constructs must meet and even cooperate if we wish to walk the path toward growth. We don't yet realize that we must learn to maintain the tension between these opposites, to be curious, and to allow that tension to hold them together, not choose one over the other.

This is why insight is so much more profound than knowledge. Insight can hold two opposing forces in tension at the same time.

The following is a letter I read at Max's funeral. Among the many ideas expressed here is that fear and joy can be in a relationship together.

Together

Dear Max,

Not many weeks go by without the memories of our childhood ripping through my mind. Among the most meaningful stories, Max, was you learning to ride a bike. You were about six years old when you were successful.

But do you remember how it started? How you learned? How you grew?

It started with you riding on the handlebars of my bike. You always wanted to go with the big kids. And one day . . . I just didn't want you to be left out, as much as you didn't want to be left out. So I propped you on my handlebars. I said "Hold on" and placed your hands on the bars so that you were centered.

Centered.

It took a while for us to get the proper balance . . . and we lagged behind the rest of the group. But it didn't matter. Through a lot of laughter—and a little yelling at each other—we figured it out.

It was only a matter of time, and we were leading the pack, with you on the handlebars, like your own little crow's nest, telling me to "Slow down," "Go faster," "Turn here," "Whoa!"

And then . . .

. . . your laughter.

You were four, Max. And you were courageous.

You also had a strong instinct to trust. I would have never ridden on those handlebars with me at the wheel.

You were courageous.

There were times I had to pick you up from daycare, a resultant occurrence of a one-parent household. I would ride my bike up the sloping hill past our school, grateful not to have to navigate the uphill climb with you on the handlebars. Then on the way home, propped in the crow's nest, you would scream loudly when we coasted down that same hill. And then . . . when we approached the bottom . . .

. . . your laughter.

The rest of the way home, you would tell me about your day in preschool. I didn't understand most of it, but I would listen. And when you weren't talking about your school, you would sing the songs that you learned there.

I hated it.

You would sing them loud.

Drawing lots of attention that an eleven-year-old didn't want.

I tried to quiet you. But you sang anyway.

I just listened.

Annoyed.

From then on, whenever I picked you up at daycare, we giggled with joy and anticipation as we approached that hill. You screamed all the way down. Admittedly, I was nervous about the speed at which we traveled some days. And at the end of the hill . . . laughter.

Both of us.

And you would talk. And sing.

And I would listen. Less annoyed each passing day.

Do you remember, Max? That's how it started. Riding a bike. Together.

You rode on my handlebars for a couple of summers, despite your clear ability to do it yourself. I think we both just enjoyed riding.

Together.

Eventually, we sat on the seat together. We steered together. When your feet reached the pedals, we added that component. And we would coast through the neighborhood. Together.

Both of us steering, you pedaling, and your long-legged brother balancing the whole unit from the back of the seat.

Finally, you did it all. Standing up on the pedals, pedaling and steering by yourself . . . and I would simply balance. Riding together.

One day while you were pedaling along on a bike much too large for you, with a seat much too tall for you . . . I hopped off the back. I simply set you free.

At first, ecstatic! You kept pedaling and talking to yourself.

And then . . .

Panic!

"Gerd! Gerd!"

I ran toward you, trying to keep up. I said, "You're doing it! Keep going! You're doing great! You don't need me!"

But you didn't see it that way, did you, Max? You had a different view from your vantage point, on a bike much too large, with a seat much too high . . .

From what I saw, Max, everything was going great! I was still with you. We were still together. In a different way. You could steer. You were a strong pedaler. And with my dead weight off the back of the bike, you now saw how strong you were. How easy it was to balance! From my perspective, everything was going perfect!

But then, as I was running alongside you, I heard you yell, "Gerd! But I don't know how to stop!"

Those words still ring loud. I don't know how to stop!

We were together in the joy, yes. But not together in the fear.

My perspective suddenly changed, Max. You were afraid. And rightfully so. The one you were trusting could no longer balance you. And balance inevitably comes to an end.

The price of growth.

I did what I could to help you.

"Gerd, but I don't know how to stop!"

"So, don't stop! Don't stop, Max. Just keep going!"

I kept encouraging you . . . all the while I, too, was panicked about how to remedy this situation.

But Max, you kept going! All the way down the block, into the cul-de-sac. And there you were . . .

Going.

In.

Circles.

Round. Round. Round.

Ten. Maybe twenty times. You were scared as hell! And with the smile of freedom, you were also filled with joy!

Smile on your face! Fear in your brow! You were alive!

And I . . . I was proud as hell.

We did the best we could. Together.

I coached you up the driveway and into the front yard grass, where your inevitable fall would incur minimal injuries. You slowed. The bike began to wobble. Balance going away.

And then. Simply. Fell over.

I ran toward you, excited!

But you were not having it."Why did you jump off!" You were angry.

"But Max, you rode by yourself! You can ride a bike!"

"Don't jump off again unless you tell me!"

With a small amount of convincing, out of your dissipating fear grew your laughter. And we laughed and talked about it for weeks. After you knew you were safe . . . the fear was gone and you were filled with joy once again!

The years went on, Max, and my listening became less. My talking became more.

I loved you. And you me. In the early years, you admired my talking. We were kids. And I felt the responsibility (or arrogance) of some good advice.

As we aged, my talking didn't cease as rapidly as your patience for it. Wisely, you stopped listening to me.

I learned a little slower.

We grew in age. Our togetherness grew less. Sometimes I wonder how much that affected you and me, both—our duration apart.

Funny thing, Max, I had to learn to ride my bike those years. Just as you were a kid, I had a kid inside me too. A kid that needed to discover my own fears. My own places to trust. My own cul-de-sac to ride in joyful, dreadful circles until I found the least restrictive crash.

Life is not the same as riding a bike—it is far more complex and nuanced.

But it's a little like it, I suppose.

It wasn't very long, Max, and I found myself on a bike much too large, with a seat much too high.

I discovered that being set free isn't all that exhilarating and that finding the least restrictive place to crash has everything to do with trust.

I'm still learning from you, Max.

Still listening.

Realizing there's more to riding than balance.

It's a harmony, really.

A harmony of work and laughter.

Trust and trial.

Exhilaration and annoyance.

Fear and joy.

From a distance, I watched as your perspective grew, your distinctive view.

You had a "Max-way" about you. It was highly magnetic. And also very confusing.

It was your "Max-way."

As adults, there were times I wanted to prop you on my handlebars again and get you centered. But I knew better. And they weren't my handlebars anymore.

Besides, we were both way too big to fit on that bike.

Our bodies. And our pride.

From you I learned that sometimes joy and fear, together, can be safe . . . like in that cul-de-sac, going round. Round. Round.

And that sometimes a person needs a few extra laps to figure out the least restrictive place to crash.

A few extra laps to learn to trust.

A few extra laps to learn to trust.

A few extra laps to learn to trust.

I learned that life might be lived in the circles of joy and fear.

But life is learned in the crash and the reflection. And that riding on the handlebars can be an exquisite place to learn.

Don't pedal too fast, Max.

It's going to take us a while to get the proper balance . . . and we'll probably lag behind.

I suspect that through some laughter—and probably a little yelling at each other—we'll get it figured out.

Don't set me free just yet.

And . . . keep talking, Max. I'm listening.

Choose Insight

Information is trivial. Insight is transformational. There is power in taking what you've learned and letting it transform you. In allowing yourself to be changed.

There is also great courage in allowing yourself to be changed. Because change involves vulnerability.

Change is frightening.

Change is uncertain.

Change is entering your wilderness, dueling with honor, and accepting two opposing forces at the same time. Fear *and* joy. Desperation *and* hope. Goodbye *and* hello.

True insight rests on your willingness to be changed.

Choose insight.

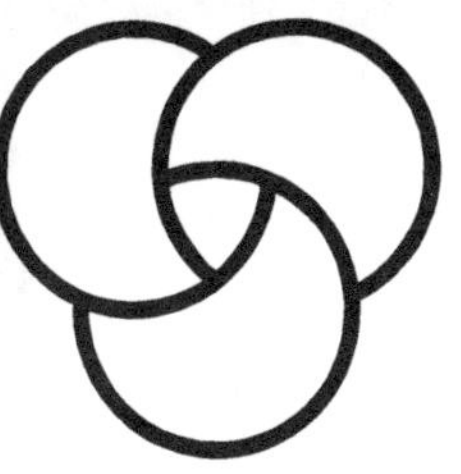

Resolving the Mystery of Autonomy

WE ARE CREATING profound space. Thus far, we've resolved the mystery of courage, which solves the illusion of confidence, replacing it with action that drives toward learning. We've resolved the mystery of insight, solving the illusion of knowledge, replacing it with transformation driving toward growth.

Now we must resolve the mystery of autonomy.

Like the other two mysteries, autonomy bears the components of an illusion, a challenge, and eventually a resolution. But this is where the similarities end.

The mystery of autonomy is different.

In my experience, people universally accept the mysteries of courage and insight with relative ease. Specifically, people don't react adversely when they learn that confidence and knowledge are illusions. Those illusions are replaced by mindset patterns that are readily embraced.

But the mystery of autonomy is different because it collides with deep-seated constructs. It'll likely alter how you understand some very basic principles of your cultural upbringing. And it'll most definitely challenge you to grow in ways you've never grown before.

In this section, we'll dissect how detrimental it is to confuse autonomy with the illusion of freedom. Then we'll discover the power that truly comes with honest autonomy.

So let's solve the mystery of autonomy.

1. The Illusion: Freedom
2. The Challenge: Self-Definition
3. The Resolution: The Three *V*s

The Illusion: Freedom

Cultures throughout the world hold freedom as a core, principal value. American culture in particular has a reverence for freedom from a holistic sociopolitical and cultural perspective.

But really, what is freedom? *True* freedom?

Do I have the freedom to drive a hundred miles per hour through downtown? How about the freedom to get on a commercial plane without going through security? How about the freedom to remodel my home to my liking, regardless of permits, inspections, and codes?

The answer to all these questions, of course, is *not really*. I mean, not without some degree of consequence and/or oversight. I cannot drive too fast through downtown without facing potential consequences. I cannot fly without TSA deeming me safe to do so. And I cannot remodel my home without an arm of government imposing certain safety restrictions on me.

Even the most basic American "freedom," the right to vote, has regulations. You cannot be a felon, you might have to register, and you might have to verify your home.

"Freedom" is relative and bound by regulations. In other words, it's an illusion.

And it's high time we shed a light on it.

Freedom—Or Something Different?

In a postpandemic culture, workplaces are immersed in an illusionary conversation about freedom. Corporations don't say "freedom" outright. Instead, they use fancy terminology, such as "hybrid work environment" and "return to premise." But ultimately, they're talking about a certain kind of restriction to freedom.

Well, I say that with hesitancy, because the conversation really isn't about freedom at all.

We all just *think* it is.

When the pandemic lockdowns began in March 2020, organizations scrambled to equip employees to work from home. This ushered in a new era of remote work the world had never seen.

In the beginning, workers and organizations alike were concerned about productivity, the ability to conduct business, and, of course, efficiency. Corporations wrestled to resolve this sudden and forced change with increased technology and other modes of social and administrative support.

There were certainly drawbacks to this work arrangement. But as we all settled in to work-from-home life, workers began to realize that there were some substantial benefits as well.

You could fold clothes during a break. You could run an occasional personal errand. You could navigate your work calendar with the use of more-efficient technology. The lack of a commute created more personal or family time.

In short, the constraints of being anchored to a workplace for eight hours or more a day, five days a week, melted away. Suddenly, people discovered what they believed was a new freedom.

Before long, companies began to call employees back to the anchored workplace. And when they did, workers resisted. We felt as though our freedoms were being stripped from us. Freedoms that we'd once never had, that we'd begrudgingly adopted, and that we now wanted to retain.

Freedom, in very basic terms, is the unmitigated ability to do what you want, how you want, when you want. Returning to the office mitigated the freedom to run to the grocery store on your lunch break, and it most certainly inhibited your desire to attend your Zoom meeting pantless!

But is *freedom* really what we're struggling with in this situation? Or is it something different?

Actually, the real construct we're dealing with here is *autonomy*. And it is different. Entirely so.

Autonomy is what I hope you'll discover if you have the tenacity to explore your profound space. It's the separation between grasping and growing. It's the true remedy to a multitude of hurdles that keep you from success and happiness.

Autonomy is everything.

Yet in many ways, it's the chief human mystery. Most of us don't even understand what autonomy *is*. We say we want it, but we don't really know what it means.

We think it means working alone, avoiding boundaries, doing whatever we want whenever we want, and having total control over our circumstances. Hence, we think *autonomy* means "freedom."

Instead, it's derived from the Greek *autonomia* (αυτονομια). It's a compound of two roots: *auto*, meaning "self," and *nomia*, meaning "law" or "custom." Put it together, and you get "self-customs."

AUTONOMY IS EVERYTHING. IN MANY WAYS, IT'S THE CHIEF HUMAN MYSTERY.

In its true form, autonomy is what allows you to cultivate, operate, and monitor a collection of self-customs or protocols in order to be true to yourself, your values, and your goals. It's the central discipline that holds together all the components of growth and progress. It's what allows you to dissolve some of the greatest barriers to success: fear, anxiety, lack of clarity, unclear boundaries, procrastination, polarized thinking, and more.

That's vastly different from unfettered freedom. In fact, true autonomy is often contrary to freedom, rubbing up against it in search of something greater, something more . . . profound.

Autonomy offers a new lens through which you can view yourself and your life. This is important because your perspective determines your trajectory and, ultimately, your destination. As Carl Jung, the father of analytical psychology, said, "I am what I choose to become."

Many people take the perspective of "Things happen to me." But autonomous people take the perspective of "I impact how things happen."

Both perspectives are valid, of course. Obviously, many things happen in life that you cannot control. However, autonomy helps you see that you actually do have *some* control, *some* power, in every situation.

Let's see how this applies to the work-from home-versus-return-to-premise situation. You may not have the privilege of choosing where you work. That decision may be outside your control. (Actually you *do* have that choice . . . but it may not be a decision you feel you can make today.) But if you have a grounded sense of autonomy, then you can develop self-customs that help you be your best self regardless of the work environment. You can *adapt* your self-customs to retain your power.

So, what perspective will you choose? Do you want life to merely happen to you? Do you want to see yourself as "lucky" or "unlucky"? Do you want to give away your power and responsibility? Or do you want to retain your power, assert ownership, have a voice, and have an impact on every aspect of your life? Do you want to understand what's in your control and what's not?

Autonomy is inherently personal, not universal. What's autonomous to you may not be so for your neighbor, your partner, your family, or your team members. And because autonomy is entirely and uniquely *you,* it isn't something that can be *given* or *granted.*

Rather, you must *grow* it yourself. And it starts by defining you who are.

The Challenge: Self-Definition

Trying to define yourself is like trying to bite your own teeth.
—Alan Watts

Alan Watts was one of the most prolific philosophers of the twentieth century. With extensive studies in the teachings of Buddhism, Taoism, and Hinduism, he acted as an interpreter to bring Eastern philosophy to the Western world.

The Eastern traditions encourage self-exploration. But Watts wasn't kidding—defining yourself is not that simple. Because *you* are not that simple.

But nobody else can be you. No one can come close to being you. It's your job—your duty—to be you. So why not be the best damn you that you can be? The most authentic you.

That means defining yourself. That means biting your own teeth.

Let's examine some background on defining yourself and then learn some tricks on how this might be done.

Differentiation of Self

Psychiatrist Dr. Murray Bowen's pioneering work on the differentiation of self—the ability to distinguish one's own thoughts and feelings from others' thoughts and feelings—has been monumental within therapeutic psychology. But differentiation of self is more than just a conceptual theory used in the psychological fields. In my experience working with people, it's also been a necessary practice for achieving personal and professional growth.

Having a healthy differentiation of self means knowing and adhering to your personal boundaries. It means recognizing where your thought ends and another person's thought begins. It's not about comparing yourself to others but making distinctions about who you are and who you are not.

Autonomy arises in the form of these personal distinctions. What makes you distinct from your neighbor, your friend, or your sibling? From your parents or your partner?

When you develop healthy self-differentiation, it makes you far less susceptible to the frequent pitfall of groupthink. It helps you abstain from exhibiting manipulative or toxic behavior as well as helps you protect yourself from such behaviors from others.

Differentiating yourself also helps you make decisions, organize your life, and accomplish your goals. For leaders, in particular, it's imperative for high performance and meaningful achievement. Defining yourself provides the necessary distance you need to establish the necessary boundaries of quality leadership.

For leaders and all individuals alike, self-definition is a key component to developing autonomy and achieving intentional growth. In other words, it's absolutely necessary for creating profound space. The kind of profound space you're looking for. The kind that helps you grow. The kind that increases your capacity for success and fulfillment.

So, what distinguishes you from someone else? Can you specifically identify what makes you unique? Can you define yourself? Can you bite your own teeth?

Actually, you define yourself all the time. Without even knowing it.

Unintentionally.

You define yourself in every meeting you attend—by showing up on time or by shuffling in late. By speaking or by remaining silent. By offering helpful insight or by offering needless distraction. By actively listening and engaging with others or by tuning out and watching the clock. By being curious to new ideas or by maintaining resistance. All of these are patterns of self-definition.

It doesn't end there. After the meeting, you define yourself by whether you follow up with directives and to-dos or shrug them off, by whether you integrate the meeting's information into your daily work or stay entrenched in your old habits, by whether you complain at the water cooler or collaborate for success. And so on.

With or without intention, you define yourself every day, with every action, with every word. Self-differentiation is best served with intention. It has been said: *If you create your intention, you create your reality. If you negate intention, you create your reality.*

So, it's time to step back and define yourself in order to then step forward into your profound space with intention. We'll do just that in the coming pages.

But first, a warning . . .

The World Is Leveraged against Defining Yourself

Creating profound space is not for the faint of heart. And self-definition is a good example of what I mean.

When it comes to defining yourself, the world is not in your favor. The world has ideas about who you are. Expectations. And the more you define yourself and become authentically *you,* the more you will bump up against this.

The great challenge to developing autonomy and self-differentiation is that most conventional social systems prefer you to be an indistinct avatar of yourself. Not because it's better for you but because it's easier for social order.

Primary school teaches you to stand in line, raise your hand, dress similar to your classmates. Order.

High school carves out a predetermined path for you—complete with postgraduate and occupation expectations—prior to your body even completing puberty. Order.

In your college years, you begin to get a taste of autonomous life. Yet you're likely grouped and housed with classmates who've "chosen" the same life pathway as you, guaranteeing you fall in line with the norms and mores of your future occupation. Order.

If you become part of the 65.7 percent of people who work at large or midsized corporations, you are expected to dress, act, and role-play like the avatar your organization needs you to be—all to maintain the organization's stability in the marketplace. Order.

Then there's the media you consume. It's their job to tell you who you are and to mold you into their perfect customer. Order.

Even your family . . . As much as they love you, they have certain expectations about who you are and who they want you to be. There's a good chance that you've lived up to their expectations from time to time and neglected your own definition in the meanwhile. Order.

Let's pause here so I can be clear: social order is not the enemy of autonomy. Social order is not the opposite of autonomy. By all means, social order is a necessary function of living in a trustworthy world.

Partly.

But social order *is* an obstacle to autonomy. A necessary one. In order to grow, you must know that you are a distinct individual, not the avatar the world demands. You may need to play the role of the avatar, but that avatar doesn't equate to who you are.

This is why defining yourself is the challenge you must face in order to resolve the mystery of autonomy.

The thing about self-definition is that it results in boundaries. Healthy ones. Autonomous ones. Necessary ones.

SELF-DEFINITION RESULTS IN BOUNDARIES. HEALTHY ONES. AUTONOMOUS ONES. NECESSARY ONES.

When you define yourself, differentiate yourself, you draw a line between you and another. A line is a separator. It creates distance between you and the expectations demanded of you.

The world will resist this. Most people live with permeable boundaries and underdeveloped self-definition, and they want you to live the same way.

Yikes.

The real trick is to learn how to define yourself, set healthy boundaries, *and* still maintain relationships. It's not easy. Hence, the fair warning.

Just know that when you define yourself, you raise the bar for all the relationships in your life. And that is always an uphill battle. *If you create your intention, you create your reality.* That goes for maintaining healthy relationships as well.

So, this is a warning, indeed. Defining and differentiating yourself is *work*. So is creating profound space.

I want you to be aware of the challenges along the way, and I want you to know you're not alone in facing them.

Now that you've been warned, let's continue developing autonomy.

Let's continue creating profound space.

The Power of *I*-Statements

If self-definition is about being intentional, then the words you choose matter greatly. That includes the words spoken aloud from your tongue as well as the words uttered silently inside your head.

It especially includes the words you use about yourself.

One way to intentionally self-define is to be aware of your *I*-statements. As with almost everything in this book, the goal is to take ownership of them.

You may be familiar with this concept. If not, an *I*-statement is simply a statement that begins with the word *I* and then follows up with a description of yourself.

As a starting point, you can practice making *I*-statements to yourself. Below, you'll find a simple but challenging exercise designed for this purpose. Ideally, you'll want to then graduate to using *I*-statements in your conversations, both professional and personal.

Why all the focus on *I*-statements? Because they're powerful. In fact, their power is fourfold. They help you discover who you are. They help you see where you're going. They help you bring authenticity to your interactions. And they help you define your values.

Power #1: *I*-Statements Define Who You Are

I-statements help you lean into what you believe, think, and feel. They help you lean into who you are.

I know what you're thinking: *Isn't it a wee bit selfish to go on and on about myself like that?*

But *I*-statements are not selfish. They are self-descriptive, self-defining, and self-enhancing. They're totally and completely in your control.

Here are some examples of how *I*-statements can define you, whether they are simple facts, voiced preferences, or deeper truths.

- I am tall.
- I am a father.
- I am a sister.
- I am afraid of heights.
- I enjoy weekends.
- I prefer tea over coffee.
- I read children's books.
- I enjoy Indian cuisine.
- I want to become a dentist.
- I love animals.
- I am smart.
- I work hard.

These are honest, meaningful statements about your attributes, your desires, and your thoughts. So if there is a fair warning about *I*-statements, this is it: they might make you uncomfortable. This is vulnerability at its finest, because you are describing yourself in no uncertain terms.

But it's just a small roadblock we all encounter on our way to genuine authenticity. Remember: vulnerability doesn't exist unless we feel somewhat exposed and uncertain.

So, be courageous. Don't shy away from exposing and expressing yourself.

Be aware, too, that while *I*-statements can be powerful, they can also be self-limiting if you define yourself too narrowly or negatively.

- Σ I am always late.
- Σ I can't stop sleeping in.
- Σ I am easily disappointed.
- Σ I am not a good reader.
- Σ I am too old to learn computers.
- Σ I don't think I'd be good at yoga.
- Σ I would love to go to Denmark, but I'm not equipped for that.
- Σ I'm too tired to finish this workout.
- Σ I don't think people like me.

Do you ever hear these self-limiting *I*-statements in your conversations or your head? If so, take a breath. Don't worry. It just means you're normal (as I already assumed you are).

These self-limiting *I*-statements come up for all of us. So what can we do?

Challenge them.

Remember, *I*-statements are not just descriptions of what you believe about yourself; they can also set or maintain the trajectory for your life. So always challenge your self-limiting *I*-statements. Question whether you truly believe them. And then decide what you want to do about it.

Believe it or not, you have the power to change the way you talk about yourself. You also have the power to describe who you will be in the future. So guess what? If you don't like your *I*-statements, you can change them.

Power #2: *I*-Statements Define Your Future

There's great power in saying "I am __________." But there's even greater power in saying "I will __________." After all, that's what growth is: knowing who you *are* today, then defining who you want to *become* tomorrow.

These types of *I*-statements are proleptic, which means they anticipate the future. They're the voice behind your vision, the voice of your intentions.

To say it another way, they draw a roadmap to whom you want to become. And the more clearly you draw that roadmap, the more likely you'll follow it.

- I will finish a marathon.
- I will complete a PhD.
- I will grow my business tenfold.

- Σ I will lose twenty pounds.
- Σ I will become an expert in my field.
- Σ I will go to Italy when I reach $1 million in sales.
- Σ I will donate $3,000 to a charity this year.
- Σ I'll figure out a way to finish this book—even if it might be hard.

Remember how I said you can change how you define yourself? Making proleptic *I*-statements is a great way to begin that process of growth. So start defining who you will be in one year, five years, ten years.

And then watch out—you just might get what you ask for!

Power #3: *I*-Statements Keep You from Trying to Define Others

Disagreements and controversy happen. Think back to a time you argued or debated with someone. How many times did you say "You __________"? And how did it go . . . ?

Well, what would happen if you said "I __________" instead?

***You*-Statements**	***I*-Statements**
You did this to me.	I wasn't prepared for this.
You're so hard to talk to.	I'm would like to explain something.
You made me do this.	I made a mistake.
You make me angry.	I feel angry.
You're wrong.	I see it differently.

In highly anxious situations, *I*-statements help you create an honest, value-based, nonaggressive stance, while still allowing you to maintain your autonomy and responsibility.

In contrast, *you*-statements raise anxiety and perpetuate conflict. They place blame and dodge responsibility. They objectify and accuse.

The problem with *you*-statements is that they attempt to define someone else. But that's not your responsibility. Your job is to define *yourself.*

So turn it around. Make an *I*-statement. Define yourself instead of the other.

When the heat rises in a conversation, self-definition can have a comforting, calming, and powerful effect on both you and the other person. Think of it this way: in the middle of a debate, an *I*-statement is undebatable. The other person cannot deny who you are nor deny what you feel or think.

Defining yourself relieves anxiety and minimizes fear. When you articulate who you are, what you believe, and what you stand for, you reground yourself in your purpose, rather than in another's demand of you.

Power #4: *I*-Statements Define Your Values

Thoughtful, intentional *I*-statements reflect not only who you are but what you value. Whether explicitly or implicitly, they reveal what's important to you.

∑ I value charity.
∑ I am generous.

- ∑ I care for others.
- ∑ I desire meaningful work.
- ∑ I give my clients my best.
- ∑ I want to grow.
- ∑ I like being with others.

As you see, you don't need to use the phrase "I value __________" in order to create this effect. As I said above, *I*-statements reveal your values both implicitly and explicitly.

And what if you don't like the values you see in your *I*-statements? Well, you can replace them with values and self-definitions that feel more . . . *you.*

This may just be one of the greatest powers of *I*-statements. They reflect your values—and your values will guide everything that is meaningful to you.

In coming chapters, we'll focus on values even more, as they're core components of autonomy and profound space. For now, though, let's start with *I*-statements, and see which direction they lead us.

101 *I*-Statements

So, are you ready to try this out for yourself? Then sit down and make a list of 101 *I*-statements.

It'll seem trivial at first. Childish, almost. But soon enough, you'll discover why defining yourself is the *challenge* of autonomy.

You may want to quit midway. Don't. Push yourself to finish. Dig deep.

Once you complete the list, you'll have discovered some new insight about yourself, and you'll have gained more clarity.

So, spend some time with the *I*-statement exercise, then step back and look at the words in front of you. What patterns do you notice? What recurring themes? Are there any negative or self-limiting statements you'd like to change?

Gleaning meaning from your *I*-statements can be a bit like decoding yourself, so be sure to read between the lines and draw out the meaning that may be under the surface. Maybe discuss it with a coach or a trusted advisor.

It's hard work but worth the effort to gain great sight into yourself. Any effort you make in taking ownership of your self-defining statements will be exponentially powerful.

I-statements will change you.

Groundwork and Foundations

Create intention, and you create your reality.
Negate intention, and you create your reality.

Being intent with your self-definition is the beginning of creating autonomy. It's the groundwork beneath the foundation of your success. Once you know your groundwork is secure, you'll always be able to rely on it. Firmly.

And if self-definition is your groundwork, then your values become your foundation. They determine not only the *stability* of your work but the *functionality* of your finished product . . . including how you determine success, failure, and fulfillment.

Let me share three stories that illustrate these points somewhat literally.

* * *

In 2014, I undertook a lifelong dream to design and build a cabin with my own hands (and with help from some friends). I didn't know whether I was capable of it, but I courageously began.

I drew plans. Spoke with architects. Redrew plans. Incorporated new ideas. Invested time, resources, and energy.

Everyone thinks the first step of a construction project is to pour a solid foundation. It's true that the foundation supports everything you plan to build upon it.

In reality, however, you can't have a solid foundation unless you have solid soil underneath it. Which means the *true* first step is to know your soil, before you pour your foundation.

We broke ground in the spring—and quickly learned that the soil was weak and unstable. It was a clay-like, soupy substance with very little integrity. We couldn't trust it. My excavating contractor dug for days. Then weeks. The soil was so poor I often saw him sitting on his excavator, shaking his head with a dumbfounded grin on his face.

We eventually replaced the entire lot with new, quality soil. It cost money and time, and it was extremely frustrating.

But it was the right thing to do. I needed to establish solid groundwork to support the foundation, which would, in turn, support everything I would build upon it.

* * *

After the groundwork had been firmly set on the cabin project, I prepared for another bucket-list item: an eighteen-day wilderness trip to paddle the entire border route of the Boundary Waters Canoe Area Wilderness in northern Minnesota. (Stay tuned: I'll include these stories in a later book.)

The timing of my trip had me leaving just before my subcontractor would pour the concrete foundation and footings. So I left my foreman with the plans, gave the team instructions to carry on in my absence, and made sure I had enough material on site to keep everyone busy.

When I returned from the wilderness trip, I was pleased to see the progress that had been made. I was also pleased to see that the cabin's foundation had been poured. Through photos, I was able to establish that the concrete person had done a fine job.

Except for one thing.

There was an error near the main entrance, where one of the supporting posts would be erected. The plans had been misread, and the foundation forms had been wrongly placed. The concrete slab was off by eighteen inches. That's a lot!

I determined that it wasn't the subcontractors' mistake. Looking at my handwritten drawings, I realized they may have been easily misinterpreted. Or perhaps my foreman misunderstood the plans? Perhaps I didn't communicate them well enough? Either way, we had a major problem.

Determining fault wasn't necessary, but solving the problem was. What could I do? Fixing the error would mean bringing the concrete company back out, which could take weeks, and we were short on time. We were also short on money, as we'd already overexpensed the groundwork.

Given the pressures of these outside forces, I started thinking about ways to work *with* the error. Was the foundation stable? Yes. Was it what I'd intended? No. But I'd drawn the original plans, and I could easily redraw them. Simple fix, right?

In the end, the cabin turned out beautifully . . . but the entry was never quite right. Was it a structural problem? No. But it was a convenience problem and an aesthetic problem. The entry was always a little too small.

I've since walked by that entry a thousand times. And every time, it's a disappointing reminder of a foundation that didn't match up to my intent. I'd spent countless hours planning how functional, beautiful, and convenient I wanted that cabin to be. I knew *exactly* what I wanted and needed. But then I compromised those plans rather than correct the unfortunate mix-up with the foundation. My foundation wasn't built to match my vision. *That* was the true error.

Had I known then what I know now, I would have found the resources and the time to fix the foundation. Your foundation supports everything you build on it. Make your foundation align with your values.

* * *

One Wednesday afternoon, I was home doing administrative tasks on a real estate venture that demanded an insane amount of work and wasn't slowing down. I received a knock at the door. A courier was standing on my front steps with a certified letter for me to sign.

Having never experienced a delivery from a courier, I thought it seemed official. Important. Businesslike. Yet a little out of place . . .

I opened the letter and was devastated by its message. I was being threatened with a lawsuit.

The key word here is *threatened*. It was an empty threat, at that.

Still, the letter might as well have said I had cancer. I panicked. I got angry. I felt hurt. I had no idea what was going on or why. I couldn't believe it.

At the time, I was over my head in my business. I'd developed a real estate investment company a few years earlier, back when the housing market was in its hangover following the 2008 crash. Homes were cheap. Foreclosures were plentiful. Everyone wanted to be a big-time real estate investor.

Everyone with a tool belt called themselves a contractor. And everyone with a paintbrush thought they could flip houses.

I owned a tool belt *and* a paintbrush. So naturally . . .

But I also had connections, work ethic, some business savvy, and a fair amount of experience. I discovered a niche of wannabe investors who were risk averse. I personally assumed the risk for them, built a general contracting company, purchased and sold real estate, and paid my investors a premium rate.

When I wasn't working on proprietary projects, I contracted my team out on a few side jobs to keep cash flow moving and my workers fed. I may have been the founder and CEO, but I was also the secretary, accountant, ditchdigger, and dishwasher. In a new start-up, that's part of business. (Or at least that's what I told myself.)

Apparently, legal threats are also part of the business.

The threat concerned one of my side projects. It was a complete renovation of a commercial building, and the owners wanted to move their professional offices there.

The thing is, this old building had a very unstable foundation. (And as you know from my cabin story above, an unstable foundation is a disaster waiting to happen.) We all knew it from the beginning—the owners, my team, and I. It was not a surprise nor a secret to anyone. We discussed the foundation's instability at great length.

Nonetheless, the owners wanted to pursue the project anyway. They were excited about making the building "pretty."

I warned them that we needed to secure several structural components and that there was quite a bit of uncertainty about what we would discover. They nodded, then started talking about kitchen cabinets and paint colors. And oh—like most people, they wanted this all on a low budget.

So from the very beginning, we didn't know how stable the foundation—or our relationship with the owners—would be. Then as our team began work, we uncovered even *more* foundational issues than we had anticipated.

One of the basement walls began to cave in. More expense, more time.

Rain came up through the floor, requiring drain tile. More expense, more time.

We couldn't fix any of these issues, though, until it stopped raining. Which it didn't. For weeks. More time, more expense.

Inspections and state requirements were slow. More expense, more time.

The back porch was falling off the building. More time, more expense.

Most of this was unforeseen. We were severely over budget, even before any of the "pretty" finish work.

As you can imagine, the owners were getting frustrated. I don't blame them. But guess who they were frustrated with?

That's right. Me.

At one point, the owners decided to take action into their own hands. They wanted to show off their building to some friends during an upcoming event, so they departed from our contract and hired someone else to finish the hardwood floors on the second level.

Directly beneath the damaged roof.

That hadn't been replaced yet.

That leaked like a sieve.

During a summer with record rainfall.

And they paid three times the going rate.

I warned them not to do it. I warned them several times, both verbally and in writing. But they were too frustrated, shortsighted, and self-indulgent to listen.

Do I have to tell you the rest of the story? It involves two inches of rain and lots of displaced blame.

These owners had a spectacular vision for their building. I mean *spectacular*. But they had a crumbling foundation and no patience to secure it. (By the way, we'll talk more about spectacular visions later, so hang on.)

Once our team completed their foundational work, the owners invited me to retire our contract—in the form of a courier's letter at my door.

I had a decision to make: *Do I pony up a large chunk of change to fight them in court, or do I walk away from the large unpaid invoice?*

The owners knew they were in the wrong and wouldn't win in court, but they also knew I didn't have the cash to contest them. This is the power of ethically questionable legal practices.

Fighting would have weakened the foundation of *my* business. I couldn't risk it. So I walked away. I paid my employees. And I spent months absorbing the deficit.

I learned three important life lessons:

1. Pretty things can distract you from foundational things.
2. Your vision is only worth the values it stands on. Your values are your foundation.
3. Always get paid up front.

PRETTY THINGS CAN DISTRACT YOU FROM FOUNDATIONAL THINGS.

Incidentally, the owners ended up finishing the project. But none of it could have happened without my team securing their foundation. And rumor has it, they had to change their vision and their plans many times in order to meet their foundational needs.

***

So there you have it—groundwork and foundations, self-definition and values.

This work is hard and it's dirty. It's not always pretty. It takes energy and effort. Most people don't have the patience for it. Just like most people want to pick out their kitchen backsplash tile, not install drain tile. But in both cases, it's necessary to do it—and to do it right.

This is what it takes to create profound space.

Once you see through the illusion of freedom and confront the challenge of defining yourself, you are ready to resolve the mystery of autonomy.

You are ready to unlock the power of your values, your vision, and your vein.

The Three *V*s.

The Resolution: The Three Vs

Articulate what's important to you. Your values.
Imagine your preferred future. Your vision.
Set your course to attain it. Your vein.

We know that self-definition is the challenge of autonomy and the groundwork for your future. But all the self-assessments and time-management hacks and efficiency protocols in the world won't mean a thing unless you know your Three *V*s: values, vision, and vein.

Knowing your Three *V*s is the core of self-definition. These three concepts work together to help you be more decisive, empower you to grow, and challenge you to stay focused.

They set you on the path to autonomy.

One *V* at a Time

When I met Rich, he greeted me with an infectious smile and one of the most welcoming handshakes I'd ever received. He had an innate ability to put a stranger at ease. His warmth, his assertive humility, and his curiosity about others was immediately perceptible.

We nestled into our booth at the café, ordered an appetizer, and began to talk. The conversation immediately propelled off the runway.

Rich told me his business was thriving. The corporation he'd helped found was branching off into uncharted territories, with investors lining up. He'd recently won an impressive award for accomplishments in his industry. All signs indicated that Rich was hugely successful.

"Rich, you seem happy," I said.

Instantly, the conversation nosedived.

Rich fell quiet. He cocked his head and lifted his shoulders in a shrug. It was an interesting gesture. A preamble.

So I questioned it. "I'm sensing 'happy' isn't the right word . . . ?"

At first, Rich did some evasive dodging. Then he finally took a deep breath.

"I used to own my company," he said. "Now I feel like it owns *me*."

With an understanding nod, I settled back in the booth as Rich shared his story.

Twenty-five years ago, Rich and his business partner knew exactly what they wanted to do: make money. So, make money they did. They began building a company from the ground up.

Rich wholeheartedly threw himself into the venture. All he could think about was landing that next sale, connecting with the next lead, and creating the lifestyle he'd always dreamed of. It filled him with a zest and drive that stretched far beyond the office walls.

"I used to get up every morning feeling hungry—hungry for the future," he told me. "I had energy. Every day, I rode my bike fifteen to twenty miles before heading to the office. Our teams were excited. We were all filled with adrenaline. Synergy. We went one hundred miles an hour."

As the years passed, the once-fledgling startup grew. And Rich's commitment to it became all-encompassing. After landing a couple of big contracts, Rich felt compelled to be all-in at the office.

"After we landed our first Fortune 500 company, that was when I knew we would make it. But in hindsight, that was also when I began to . . . I don't know . . . lose my place, I guess. I became a no-show at family functions. I stopped seeing my friends. It really tested my wife. She was supportive—she knew how much I wanted this business to succeed. But I know it was still hard on her. I just wasn't home as much. My normal workday went from eight or nine hours to ten to twelve. And when I was home, my mind was still at work. Not in a bad way. I mean, it was exciting. But . . ."

The months became years, and the years became decades. In twenty-five years, the hopeful startup had grown into an industry standout. This was great in many ways. But not so great in others. Rich was suddenly becoming aware of some things that bothered him about his commitment to the job.

"The more the company grows, the more weight I feel," Rich admitted. "I don't come into the office each morning with energy. It's more like obligation. I feel henpecked by deadlines and routine. I'm annoyed by our employees and vendors—people I used to enjoy. All I'm doing is going through the motions, but even that feels like too much. It's the same feeling every day. Every . . . single . . . day."

Rich reached for his soda, took a quick sip, then slowly set the drink down.

"But it's not like I want the old days back," he said. "I mean, I do sometimes miss all that adrenaline and creativity. But I don't think I could keep up with that pace these days—I'm not in my twenties anymore." He sighed. "It's weird. I don't want what I used to have, yet I don't want what I have now. Even the money isn't as exciting as it used to be . . ."

With that, Rich grew quiet. I waited patiently as he gazed out the café window, thinking.

"Something's different now," he finally said, still looking out the window. "It's hard to explain. I guess I'm just not feeling it. I still want this business, but I want something different for my life. I don't want this business to run my life anymore."

I nodded once again.

I regularly encounter people like Rich. They're high achievers. They're successful by many standards. Yet they feel unfulfilled. Consumed. Drained. Unhappy. Bored. Miserable. Grasping.

These are all signs of frail autonomy. Or at least unclear, muddied autonomy.

Working together, Rich and I set a goal to help him clear his muddied autonomy and reclaim a sense of ownership over his life. That is, we resolved to clear this mystery one *V* at a time.

Values

Twenty-five years ago, Rich knew exactly what he valued: money, excitement, and building business. So he aligned his life to that value. He was energized, happy, fulfilled. Until he wasn't.

As Rich and I worked together, he came to realize that the company wasn't the only thing that had grown over two and a half decades. He realized he had grown as well.

No wonder Rich was unhappy. The life he'd built no longer fit him. Perhaps better said, he'd built a life based on his company's demands rather than his evolving values. There was a disparity between what his business needed from him and what he wanted for himself. The achievements and accolades he'd garnered over the years weren't enough to overcome the disparity. Rich's company had started to define Rich.

"I know I own this company," he said, "but I feel like my company owns me."

Rich was successful at business, but unsuccessful at being Rich.

To move forward, he needed to redefine his life. With intention. And to do that, he needed to clearly understand his values.

With some help and some lengthy conversations, Rich drew distinctions between his old values and his current values. He determined that many of his values hadn't changed over the years. He was still committed to his business, and he still believed in what he sold. He still valued his support system: his wife, business partners, and close friends and family.

But Rich also determined that some of his values had changed drastically over the course of nearly three decades.

Rich desired a more regulated workday. He wanted to release some control of his day-to-day business oversights. With some humility, he admitted that he longed for what he calls flextime. In his younger years, Rich had used this tongue-in-cheek term to ridicule anyone who didn't fit his narrow definition of work ethic.

Vision

Rich's new values started to pour a solid foundation upon which he could build his vision.

What is a vision? Literally, it's an imagination of a future life you can "see." In this case, Rich imagined a vision of fulfillment, of growth, and of a life he had never painted before.

Rich's vision included broad goals, such as bold business growth and further expansion. But it also included simple pleasures Rich had historically overlooked: dinners at home with his family, regular vacations, and simple plans to achieve some bucket-list items.

Every year, I meet thousands of people who say they want to succeed yet have no idea what "success" looks like to them. At best, they think success looks like what someone else tells them it should look like.

But success is relative. Success is relative to *your* vision. Your vision paints the picture of your success. It's an image of what your values and goals could look like if you lived them fully.

When Rich started his company, he'd armed himself not with a vision but with an idea: to create a company that would make him money. That idea came to fruition . . . but then the company behind that idea took over his life. Even when his values evolved, he found himself trapped in that old idea, unable to see a clear picture of how he fit into it.

So as Rich and I worked together, he cast a new vision. Not for his company but for his whole life. He began to paint a picture of what his values and goals looked like to him when they were lived fully.

Suddenly, he could envision what it looked like to own his company but not let it own him. He could see himself enjoying his workday, free from mundane decisions. And he could see his time being reallocated to family, friends, and his personal endeavors.

Once Rich painted this vision, he realized that the only way to make it reality was to make different decisions. Decisions about how he would live. It would involve sacrifice.

Remember—success means leaning into vulnerability and taking courageous action, while failure is often the avoidance of vulnerability. Well, Rich leaned into the vulnerability and became courageous.

Rich's broader vision demanded that he become a different kind of employer, one who delegated tasks, made difficult decisions, and held himself accountable. It demanded that he become a different kind of spouse, one who kept his commitments. And as you can imagine, it demanded that he become a different kind of business partner and father and neighbor and so on.

But Rich was focused on a new kind of success—one that involves change and vulnerability.

Vein

Rich's clear values allowed him to paint a clear vision of his preferred future. Now, he needed to begin working toward that future. He needed to focus on the third *V*—his vein.

Inside the body, a vein is a little vessel that does big work. It leads blood to the heart.

When it comes to self-growth, your vein leads your actions toward your goal. Your vein consists of little decisions—daily routines, habits, actions, conversations, boundaries, attitudes, and self-talk—that have big results. If you align your vein with your values and vision, it can lead you toward growth and fulfillment. If you don't align them, however, it can lead you toward grasping and misery.

Rich came to understand that he had been trapped in a vein of actions leading to an old vision and old values. It was leading him to nothing but more of the same. More unfulfilled moments in an imbalanced life. More days filled with boredom, powerlessness, and frustration.

So, it didn't take long for Rich to realize that if he really wanted to move toward his new vision, he needed to create new actions. He needed to adopt a new vein.

It wasn't easy. As committed as he was to his values and vision, he still found it very challenging to adopt the new behaviors in his new vein.

For instance, learning to delegate his responsibilities at the office was difficult. While many people are happy to unload work responsibility, Rich had a hard time trusting that the work would get done. Likewise, it took Rich a while to learn how to schedule his day and his life now that he'd embraced flextime.

Creating profound space took time. But Rich kept working at it. He kept his future vision clearly in front of him, and he kept reminding himself of the values underneath it all. And as he did, the challenges slowly eased. He began to adopt his new vein. He began to live a profound life.

More importantly, Rich reclaimed his autonomy. He reclaimed his ability to maintain the routines and self-customs he believed were important. Rich increasingly felt in control of his life. His business no longer owned him.

Or as Rich put it: "My life belongs to me now."

And now it's your turn. Now it's time to push past your preambles, create your profound space, and take a close look at your values, vision, and vein. This is what you must do to resolve the mystery of autonomy.

Helping You Define Your Three *V*s

Does Rich's story resonate with you? Can you relate to it in even a small way?

Maybe you know that feeling of grasping for something hard to name. Maybe you want to change something, but you don't know what. Maybe you desire a new way of life but don't fully know what actions to take to get there. If so, you need to redefine your *V*s.

Or maybe you don't resonate much with Rich's story because, unlike him, you've *never* felt fulfilled. Maybe his story made you suddenly realize that you've *never* given any of this any thought over the years. In that case, you need to define your *V*s for the first time.

Wherever you are on your pathway, defining your three *V*s will help you create the profound space necessary to set your course toward autonomy and fulfillment.

So, who are you? What's important to you? *What are your values?*

Where do you want to go? What is your goal, purpose, objective, or destination? What does it look like? *What is your vision?*

How will you move toward your values and vision on a daily basis? How will you live, work, and play? What are your behaviors and boundaries? *What is your vein?*

Go deep with these questions. Be intentional. Be bold enough to create the profound space necessary to really change your life.

Think about your answers and then write them down. Seriously. WRITE THEM DOWN. Express your three *V*s as a statement, a narrative, or a tagline. Whatever helps you makes this real, tangible, attainable.

The Three *V*s are a great way to begin the process of defining yourself. This construct will help you become clearer about what steps and actions you need to take to hone your autonomy.

But remember: autonomy is about self-customs, not about the illusion of freedom. In fact, it's *all* about self-customs.

To develop and grow your autonomy, you must begin to label the self-customs that make you the best you. And they will, at first, make you feel *not* free. But eventually, your self-customs will create more freedom than you can imagine.

Self-Customs

I wake at 5:00 a.m. daily. Sometimes earlier.

The first hour belongs to me. I read. I write. I meditate. I do whatever I need to do to prepare for my day. Then I go work out at my local gym.

I do this at least five days a week.

Some days, I'm actually excited to go to the gym. From the moment I wake up, I'm excited, full of energy, anticipating the workout. I know it'll be good for me.

Other days, I simply don't want to work out. I don't feel motivated. My energy is low. Even in that first hour, while I'm journaling or reading, I find myself wishing I didn't have to go to the gym. I just don't want to do it.

So, at least five mornings a week, it's more or less a coin flip: Am I excited to go to the gym or not?

But heads or tails, I go to the gym anyway. Without fail. Even if it's begrudgingly. Even if I make it only twenty minutes instead of the usual hour.

And every time, after I'm done, I am grateful.

Every time.

I'm not trying to gain or lose weight. I'm not trying to run a certain distance or lift a certain number of pounds. I'm simply moving my body. It's not rocket science.

You see, I've learned that I'm a better person when I work out regularly. I'm more patient. I'm nicer to the people around me. I like myself more. I have more respect for myself—especially when I complete a workout on one of those unmotivated mornings.

I work out because it makes me a better me. It makes me the best me.

And that's huge.

Working out is one of my self-customs. Remember when we talked about this earlier? If you recall, "self-custom" is literally what the word *autonomy* means. These are the laws or customs you hold for yourself. Both to limit yourself and to maximize your potential.

Working out is just one of my self-customs. I have a multitude of others: reading, journaling, writing, meditating, dating my wife, seeing my friends regularly, going for a walk in the woods, being an informed consumer of food, turning off my phone and computer hours before bedtime, and more. These are my personal self-customs. I have some for my work life too.

This is what autonomy is. It's putting your Three *V*s into action. It's building a life catered around what you need to do to make yourself a better person. It's knowing yourself in a new way and ultimately taking action to make yourself the best you, you can be.

There was a time in my life when I wasn't as good at autonomy, when I wasn't as good at creating self-customs. Maybe you feel like you're in that time of your life right now.

Certainly, there are obstacles. Maybe you're a parent and a spouse and a professional and a volunteer. If so, much of your time is taken up by serving, by caring for others, and just by everyday life. That happens.

In fact, that happens way too often.

This is why it's even more important that you resolve the mystery of autonomy. That you create self-customs to help you be the best you can be. To be the best worker you can be. The best family member and friend you can be. Your autonomy and your self-customs help every aspect of your life.

It's important to emphasize that self-customs are not *hobbies*. It's true that certain activities—such as reading and writing—can be hobbies for some people and self-customs for others. It's not the *what* that distinguishes a hobby from a self-custom but the *why*.

A hobby is a fun activity you occasionally do in your free time, for the sake of leisure. A self-custom is a personal "law" you always follow for the sake of self-improvement and growth. It's a discipline, a promise, a commitment, a need—not a pastime. It is a custom to live by that makes you a better you.

For instance, I surf when I travel, but I lift weights regularly to stay healthy. I read mystery novels for enjoyment, but I read research papers and nonfiction to help me be the best consultant I can be.

You might eagerly look forward to your self-customs with joy (as I do half my workouts). Or you may begrudge them (as I do the other half of my workouts). But either way, they will all eventually bring you a great amount of joy and satisfaction, because you've followed through on promises you've made to yourself.

Now, I know what you might be thinking: *This all sounds great on paper, but I'm barely making it through the day and the week as it is. Now you're telling me to add even* more *to my to-do list? Why in the world would I do self-customs?*

Let's turn that around: Why in the world *wouldn't* you do them? Self-customs don't take from you; they add to you. If an activity makes you feel better and makes you a better person, why *not* do it? What stops you from taking action to be a better person?

Sure, all of us have lazy days from time to time. All of us have days when we need to just give ourselves a break (which, by the way, can be a self-custom in itself). All of us have those moments when we don't feel like getting off the couch, putting on our workout clothes, and heading to the gym. Or when we don't feel like turning off Netflix, grabbing our journal, and finding a quiet spot in the house.

Catch the key word there? It's *feel*. Self-customs aren't about feelings and emotions. Or at least they're not about letting feelings and emotions keep you from becoming the person you want to be.

So, what are *your* self-customs? If it helps, look back at what you wrote for your Three *V*s. What self-customs rise to the surface as you think about your values, vision, and vein?

Decide to put the excuses down.

Decide to respect yourself.

Decide to *do* it.

Choose Autonomy

Before takeoff on a commercial airliner, the crew gives direct instructions for what to do in a worst-case scenario. They explain that if air pressure in the cabin changes, air masks will drop down from the cabin storage. They instruct you to put on your own mask first, before helping those around you.

Why? Because without oxygen, you are quickly rendered useless. Until you help yourself, you are no help to others.

That's autonomy. Your oxygen.

Your family, your office, every marketing influencer and advertiser, and just general social order—they all want you to behave in a certain manner that benefits them. But what benefits *you*? So, what gives *you* oxygen?

Structure your self-customs to benefit you, and then stick to them. That happens when you solve the mystery of autonomy. You give yourself oxygen.

So, choose your self-customs and leverage your Three *V*s. If you don't, someone else will choose them for you. They'll give you *their* customs and expectations. They'll tell you it's "freedom," but it'll be the exact opposite. You'll discover that you're living in complete obligation. Your life will own you, like Rich's company owned him.

But you can change that.

Choose autonomy. You'll be glad you did. And you'll grow in it every day.

Bringing It All Together

WE'VE SPENT THE better part of this book exploring the three mysteries of courage, insight, and autonomy. So now, in this final section, it's time to bring it all together so you can understand not just the mysteries but the profound space in a tangible, recognizable way.

We'll begin by discussing how you can leverage each mystery to create a dynamic harmony of profound space. And then we'll bring the book to a close by returning to where it all started . . . the cigar box.

Let's get to it.

Leveraging the Three Mysteries

By now, I hope you understand that each mystery is powerful on its own.

But here's what you maybe don't yet know: when you bring two mysteries together, they each become even more powerful. And when you bring all three mysteries together—with intention—they unlock the dynamic environment we've been building toward. The mindset and the way of life that is profound space.

Perhaps we can best understand the relational nature of the three mysteries via a Venn diagram. Each circle represents a mystery.

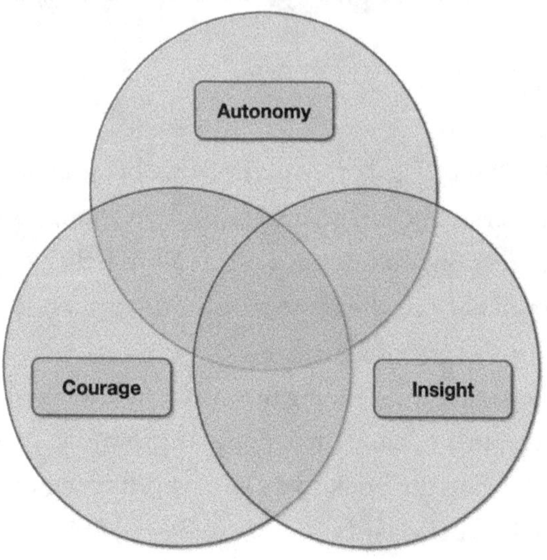

As with any Venn diagram, the overlapping areas are of key importance. These are the ways the mysteries work together and enhance one another. In the very middle, you'll see how all three mysteries unify.

So let's deconstruct this Venn diagram and then build it back together. As we do, we'll discover that one mystery stands above the rest as the true key to profound space. And that's autonomy.

But first, let's look at how courage and insight work on their own and together.

Leveraging Courage and Insight

How does it look and feel to leverage courage and insight in your life? Let's paint a portrait.

Courage

People who master courage participate in two powerful activities: actionable risk-taking and reflection. Because of this, they're likely innovative, trying new things and looking for new solutions. Their ability and willingness to problem solve will also be strong, and their perseverance to reflect on their actions will keep them on the path to gaining confidence through experiential learning.

Courageous people have a deep connection to vulnerability and fear. This benefits them if they recognize their vulnerabilities and use them to grow. In this case, their fears won't hold them back. Rather, these people can embrace their vulnerabilities and disassemble their fears in order to accomplish their goals.

That said, some courageous people may use risk-taking action to avoid their fears and vulnerabilities rather than understand and embrace them.

Insight

People who are strong in insight are very curious. They are open to new information, and they readily learn new ideas and strive to put them into practice. They maximize the transformative nature of insight. They are comfortable in a dynamic environment, where curiosity flourishes and change is commonplace. Insightful people are open and looking for ways to become and to grow.

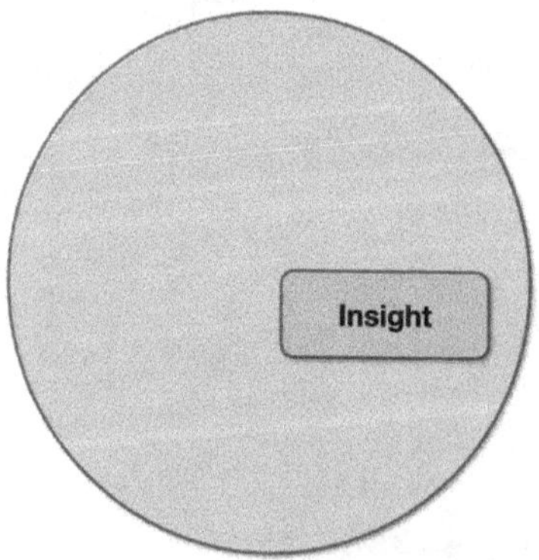

However, some insightful people can spin their wheels when it comes to long-term-goal accomplishment. Because their nature is to change with ease, which means they may easily get distracted and pulled off their course of progress.

Courage and Insight Together

If courage and insight are impactful on their own, then leveraging them together is even more powerful.

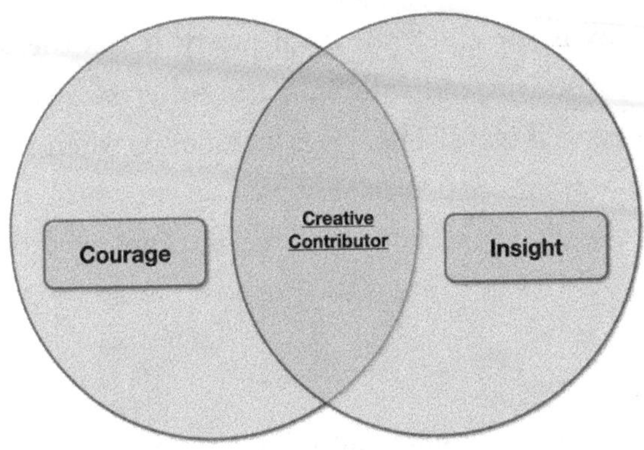

When courageous people also grow in their capacity for insight, they become creative contributors. They combine risk-taking action with curiosity—a mix that flourishes in hyper-dynamic environments that value new ideas. The combination of courage and insight gives people a tremendous ability to learn *and* effect change in both themselves and others. Others often benefit from the creative ideas that follow.

When people combine these two mysteries, they also become more thoughtful and calculated, which lowers the "risk" of their actions. This in turn builds certainty and trust as well as lowers anxiety in a group or organization.

Clearly, insight and courage are important individually and in tandem. But even together, these two mysteries are not enough to create the true harmony of profound space.

This is where autonomy comes in.

Leveraging Autonomy

Autonomy is the chief human mystery. It has the unique power to inform and influence the other two mysteries in exponential ways. This gives autonomy, when properly understood, a more powerful impact on your success.

Let's begin by painting a portrait of autonomy on its own. Surprisingly, it's not always the prettiest picture . . .

Autonomy

People who have mastered autonomy know themselves well. They take ownership in their identity, their life, and their work. They feel both authority and accountability in equal measure, and they have the initiative to be their best selves.

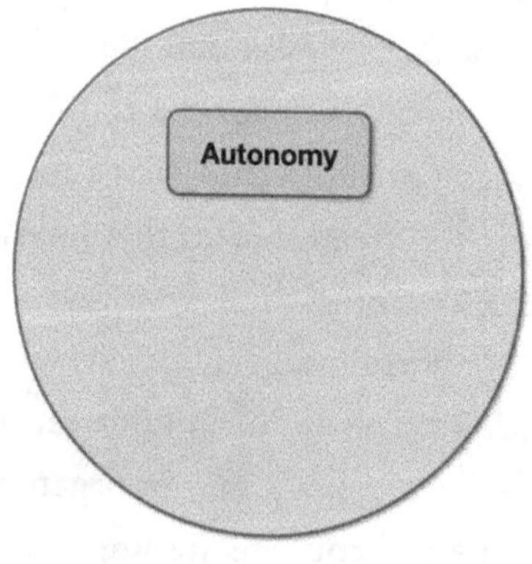

However, autonomy absent of courage or insight can become the act of turning inward on yourself. On its own, autonomy has the power to destroy and isolate the self.

It's like a cancer cell.

A healthy cell in the human body knows its job: it grows, works, divides, then dies. The key is that it takes direction from the body. It's receptive to feedback and will respond accordingly.

A cancer cell is different. It doesn't take direction from the body. It won't respond to feedback in its environment. It just grows and divides uncontrollably. It actively avoids the immune system. It fails to do its job.

Unchecked autonomy can become like a cancer cell. It refuses the insight of transformation. It fears so much that it represses courageous action. It denies vulnerability. It avoids accountability. It takes no risk. It remains closed. It denies newness.

Essentially, unchecked autonomy rebels against the system intended to help it grow. It rebels against profound space.

Autonomy without courage and insight can make people toxic to themselves and to others. There's an old proverb that says, "Most people die at twenty-five but just aren't buried until they're seventy-five." This might be easily attributed to the person who develops a strong but stagnant autonomy, void of courage and insight.

Again, autonomy is the chief mystery, with exponential power. But its power must be balanced with insight and courage. This is how we build not just harmony but profound space.

Autonomy and Insight Together

Without autonomy, insight has very little direction. With autonomy, though, insight can set a proper destination and tangible boundaries.

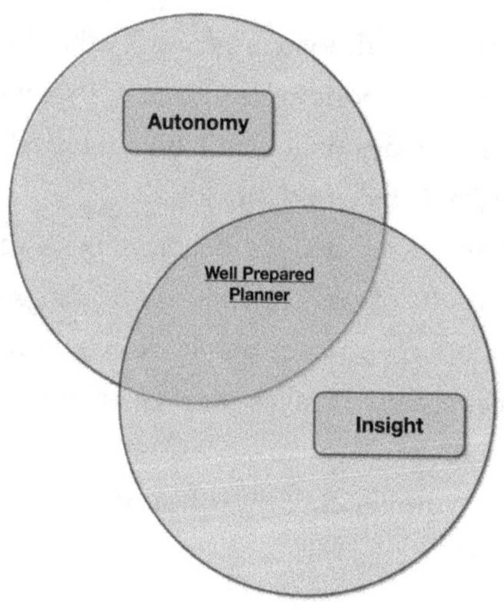

People who are strong in both insight and autonomy are well-prepared planners. They know themselves and their direction. They don't change just for the sake of change; they have clear vision and integrated rationale. There's a strong sense of ownership and accountability.

In addition, these people also have the openness to ask curious questions and the willingness to be transformed by the process. Insight and autonomy, together, improve the desire to succeed.

Autonomy and Courage Together

Courage without autonomy also lacks definitive direction. But when people pair courage with autonomy, they become efficient actors because they can focus their courageous action on a specific end result. In other words, there is purpose behind the action.

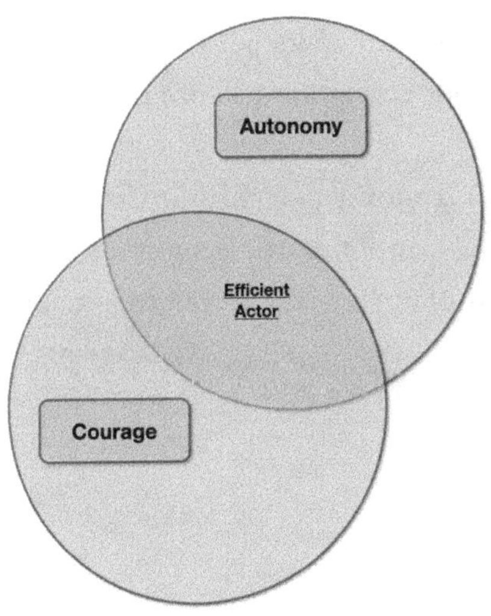

Their action-oriented risk-taking will move in a clear, motivated direction. This kind of efficiency *gets things done.* With autonomy and courage, people check off tasks with relative eagerness.

So, are you starting to see how it all works now? Each mystery, individually, has benefits yet also limitations—in the case of isolated autonomy, severe limitations. One mystery alone cannot fulfill the full picture that is profound space.

Let's keep going on this track. Let's see what happens when we pair two mysteries . . . but leave out the third.

Leveraging Two—But Not Three—Mysteries

When it comes to combining two mysteries, the whole is greater than the sum of its parts. But as you will see, two mysteries are not enough to balance the entire equation.

Insight and Autonomy . . . without Courage

If you recall, people with insight and autonomy are well-prepared planners. Whatever they do, they carry out extremely well.

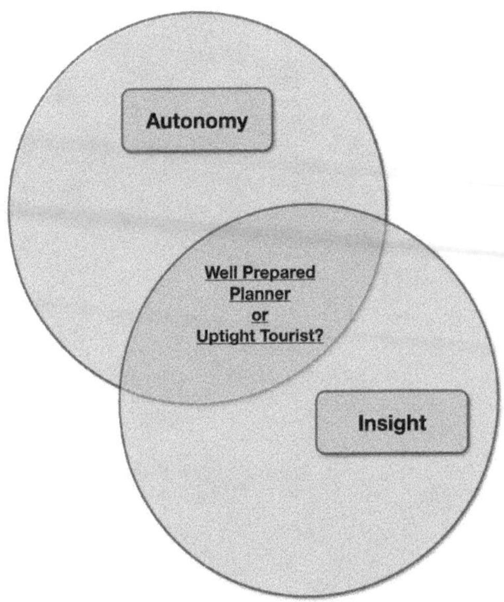

But without courage, they may never become actual participants. They may prefer to plan a journey for someone else . . . while they themselves, like upright tourists, remain in the hotel, viewing the city from a distance.

They may like the *idea* of trying new things, but they don't like the risk associated with *actually doing* something new. They resist active engagement because they fear the vulnerability involved.

Courage and Autonomy . . . without Insight

People with courage and autonomy are efficient actors. They're goal directed . . . but they may not make the wisest decisions if they lack insight.

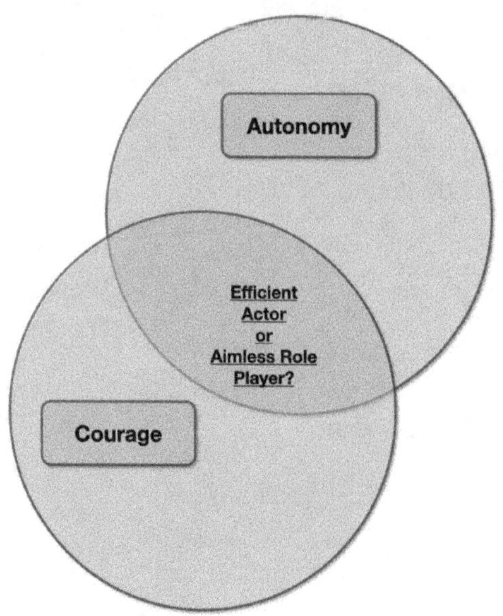

These people may become worker bees who check off all the boxes on their to-do lists but learn nothing new along the way. Therefore, they may find themselves spinning their wheels, doing the same thing for years with mediocre results. Without the ability to absorb new insight, they won't be transformed by their experience or open to growth. (Think Kodak.)

Courage and Insight . . . without Autonomy

Creative contributors have a combination of courage and insight . . . but without autonomy, they might lack definitive direction.

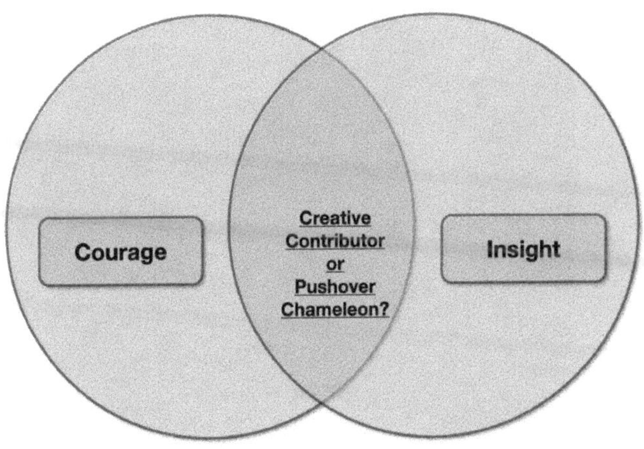

These people can become chameleons. They can readily adapt to solve problems and initiate new action, but they have trouble making decisions and setting boundaries. Taking responsibility is also a challenge for them.

Chameleons are driven by action—but not necessarily by results. They move from idea to idea without the persistent focus or the tenacity to finish a goal.

Courage *and* Insight *and* Autonomy Together

At last, we can join all three circles of our Venn diagram.

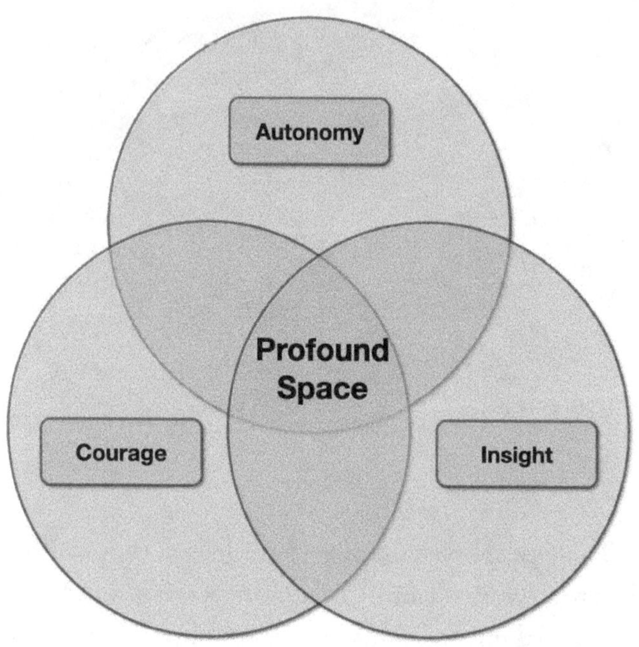

When you hold the mysteries of courage *and* insight *and* autonomy in harmony, you create space. Not physical space but profound space.

Profoundly transformational. Profoundly innovative. Profoundly intuitive. Profoundly sensory. Profoundly belonging to you.

Let's paint the full portrait.

Creating Profound Space

So what does it look and feel like to harmonize all three mysteries and create profound space? In my time as a consultant and coach-practitioner, I've observed this phenomenon in many people.

When people create profound space, they have the unique capacity to listen with their eyes and articulate with their expressions. Their sense of self is palpably present without being dominating. They convey emotional courage that inspires others. Their confidence comes from a long line of failures, and their wisdom comes from trial and error.

Anyone can dwell in profound space. And if you do, you will unlock your own unique capacity to maintain healthy relationships, find meaning in your work and your life, and grow to become a better version of yourself every day.

Consequently, you'll also unlock the character traits corporations and team leaders seek in employees:

- Σ Innovation, calculation, actionable risk-taking, problem-solving, continual learning, and perseverance are directly related to solving the mystery of courage.
- Σ Openness, curiosity, adaptability, and dynamism are directly correlated with solving the mystery of insight.
- Σ Ownership, initiative, authority, flexibility, discipline, and accountability are clear results of solving the mystery of autonomy.

Desirable traits such as these don't just magically appear. These traits—and more—are the results of creating profound space. They are the results of growth.

Profound space allows you to become better at what you do and better at who you are. But as you know by now, it takes real work. It requires you to push beyond your preambles.

So let's return to the beginning, shall we?

My Cigar Box, Revisited

The tie clip . . . the bandana . . . the collar tabs . . . the cuff links . . . the cigar box itself . . .

As we conclude our journey, let's explore this profound space once again.

* * *

The tie clip . . .

My grandfather died in 1978. Fell over dead. Heart attack. I was eighteen months old.

Family stories tell me that he'd served as a spy for the US military in Germany during World War II. He'd grown up in a German-speaking American household, so he was handed a Nazi uniform and ordered to blend in.

My grandmother says he returned home a *different man.* Changed. I believe her. I imagine it would be difficult to return to a regular life at home after wielding a weapon against your first cousins and spying on an enemy in dangerous situations.

Given the technology and sociological stereotypes of the postwar era, it's fair to presume that mental health was not a priority for my grandfather. As a result, hypertension, obesity, and cardiovascular issues grasped hold. Likely some depression and anxiety mixed in as well.

But who's to say for sure? The man had never darkened the door of a doctor's office, despite having multiple problematic symptoms. So, eventually, the heart attack killed him. Or was it PTSD? Or his weight? Or perhaps he simply died in battle—thirty years after the war.

The relationship bonds he left behind were . . . confusing. He had enigmatic charisma, a swirling mystery of dynamic, painful, energizing capability. He was one of eighteen children, and over the years, each of his remaining siblings say the same thing: "Your grandpa and I were the closest of us all."

Yet closeness and intimacy were not characteristics his own children would attribute to him. In their experience, he often treated close family like strangers, while he gave strangers what warmth he could muster.

I believe my grandfather was a good man but a damaged man. I believe he silently suffered from emotional and cognitive experiences I can't comprehend. And though I empathize with his story, I also recognize that it is the genesis of generational dysfunction. His pain was given to and shared by those who followed.

My job is not to fix this for my grandfather nor for anyone else. That's not possible. My job is to write a different story for my own life and to give my kids a different perspective. That's challenging enough!

And so I keep this tie clip close. It's a tangible reminder of my past and a personal expectation of my future.

It's my aim to end generational dysfunction for my branch of the family tree. It's not about being perfect but being on the path toward healing. It's not about fixing life but giving life a new trajectory.

It means I must move from grasping to growing.

It means I must create profound space.

I must act with courage and face my own vulnerability. I must risk failure, embrace learning, and eventually grow into confidence.

I must confront my wilderness and turn information into insight. I must accept that who I am today is not who I will be tomorrow—and that such change is not a betrayal of myself or my family of origin but rather a sign of me becoming *more* me.

I must continue to nurture my autonomy. I must follow my values, my vision, and my vein in order to discover something much deeper than freedom.

It is for all these reasons that I keep my grandfather's tie clip in my cigar box. It reminds me of the drastic need to create profound space. For me and for my family's future.

The tie clip . . .

***

The bandana . . .

At roughly eighteen years old, my youngest brother, Max, began experimenting with drugs. Cocaine mostly.

The experimentation became a habit. The habit became a lifestyle. The lifestyle became a secret.

A secret few people knew.

A secret that demanded isolation.

A secret that was released from its isolation only after Max's death—an unfortunate parallel to Max himself.

The story goes, Max was six months cocaine-free when he died. But even then, he was still seventeen years deep into addiction.

I suspect he'd faced multiple precipice moments over those years and had dipped into the waters of his own wilderness from time to time. But too many masters had lorded over him for too long. Those masters had slowly and methodically done their damage.

I keep Max's shredded bandana as a reminder that masters can cause irreparable damage. I keep it as a reminder to own my masters before it is too late. And I keep it to remind me to create the kind of profound space where falling off a bike can be a beginning or an ending . . . and it's my choice how to interpret the fall.

The bandana . . .

* * *

The cuff links . . .

Why do I even have them?

In order to answer that, we need to back up a bit.

I grew up in a family of six. We weren't *dirt* poor. On the ladder of wealth, our family had a rung. It may have been the lowest rung, but it was a rung nonetheless.

I say this because I've always been somewhat proud of the little means by which I learned to live. Hand-me-down clothes were a necessity. Negotiating groceries was commonplace. Family vacations were sparse.

I watched closely as my mom and dad each pinched and saved in different ways. They often worked multiple jobs. They knew that planning ahead was an absolute must. And because they planned responsibly and avoided frivolity, we always had food, heat, and lights. And sometimes a little more.

I entered college in 1995. My first year, I lived on $100 per month—money I had saved in advance. My second year, I figured out how to drop it to $50 per month. The pinch was partly a game of pride and partly a necessity. I never worried about money because there wasn't much to worry about.

So that's how I paid for college and two graduate degrees: I had scholarships and grants. I had loans. I worked my ass off. And I rarely invested in frivolity.

I was proud of that.

By 2005, I was preparing to graduate from my second master's degree program and start a new job that would pay me a whopping $39,000 a year. With my graduation ceremonies quickly approaching, I entered a store to buy a white dress shirt. My budget was fifty dollars—the same amount as my monthly budget my sophomore year of college.

Best laid plans . . .

A young salesman led me over to the French cuff shirts. He told me they were coming back in style—and not just as formal wear. He was very convincing.

I liked the idea of wearing something a little different from the norm. I get bored with same-old-same-old clothing. I've never been flashy, by any means. But once in a while, I like something unique.

I was sold on the French cuff shirt. But with a French cuff shirt come cuff links. You can't avoid it.

So, I walked into the store with a $50 budget for a standard white dress shirt; I walked out of the store with a $90 white French cuff shirt and $50 cuff links. I got talked into something outside of my comfort zone. But for the first time in years, I spoiled myself.

Sometimes you have to indulge and reward yourself, especially when you've earned it.

Sometimes you just have to be happy that life is yours to enjoy.

Sometimes you have to defy your boundaries in order to learn how to respect them again.

Sometimes you have to jump off the back of the bike and see what happens next.

Sometimes you have to bring home the family-size package of Oreo cookies, even if your body will hate you for it later.

Sometimes you have to buy the $100 bottle of wine to learn it tastes twenty times better than the $20 bottle.

Sometimes you have to dive naked into the Costa Rican Pacific on a deserted beach on New Year's Eve. Just because.

Sometimes you have to stand in awe of a routine sunrise and be happy you are alive.

Sometimes you have to bring your spouse flowers for no reason at all.

Sometimes you have to fail miserably in life, business, and relationships, only to discover yourself more fully and to understand that life after failure is even better than life before it.

Stop and read that again: *life after failure is even better than life before it.*

You learn gratitude after failure. After loss. After stupidity. After mistakes. After frivolity. After saddling yourself with cuff links for that French cuff shirt you just had to buy after getting yourself through college and two graduate programs.

Every decision has a consequence—good, bad, or in between. You often have to just *do the thing,* discover its consequence, then learn from it. Life requires leaps into the wilderness.

But most people don't like this. They refuse to leap. They're filled with fear. They grasp for stability and order.

That's not living. That's simply *existing.*

The world is dense with these exist-ers. In fact, many of them are the ones setting the arbitrary rules for you, me, and the rest of the world.

You don't have to be an exist-er.

You don't have to listen to them.

So buy the French cuff shirt.

The cuff links . . .

***

The collar tabs . . .

Every day I wear those damn collar tabs. Every day they bring me back to my cigar box of profound space. Every day they mold my memories, my thoughts, and my motivations.

Every day.

Think about the things you do every day. Or better yet, pick something new to do every day, then watch what happens.

But choose wisely. What you do every day determines who you become.

WHAT YOU DO EVERY DAY DETERMINES WHO YOU BECOME.

You become a runner by running every day. Not by winning. Not by racing. Not even by improving. You become a runner by *running*. Every day.

You become a writer when you write every day. You become a hiker when you hike every day. See how this works?

You become a giver when you give every day. You become a smiler when you smile every day. You become a collaborative coworker when you collaborate with your coworkers every day.

Now let's try something a little more complex. You become a parent when you parent every day. Same goes for being a partner or a lover.

We forget sometimes that relationship words are nouns based on verbs. Which means we need to see our relationships as not just titles but actions we must take.

Every day.

Of course, I say "every day" only as an illustration, an exaggeration to hammer the idea home. Case in point, I don't use my collar tabs *every* day. I opt for the occasional sweater on workdays, and I wear T-shirts on the weekends.

But still—I do wear dress shirts a lot. Which means I need those collar tabs a lot. Which means I go into that cigar box a lot. Which means I enter my profound space a lot.

Let's round it up and call it "every day."

And while we're at it, let's talk about what happens if you *don't* do something every day.

Can you call yourself a runner if you don't run every day? Can you call yourself a lover if you don't love every day? Can you call yourself a friend if you don't treat your friends well every day? Can you call yourself a spouse if you disregard your spouse every day?

Can you—

I think you get the point.

So, choose to do something every day and watch what happens. Choose to do something that moves toward your goals, and watch what happens.

But once again, choose wisely.

The collar tabs . . .

* * *

The tie clip . . . the bandana . . . the cuff links . . . the collar tabs . . . the cigar box itself . . .

In a sense, we all have a cigar box. A space where we store meaningful items. A space where we store thoughts we haven't made sense of yet and ideas that make us a little uncomfortable.

Often that space is not physical but emotional. That space is profound. So profound that we feel compelled to guard it with preambles, the stories we tell ourselves and others. We believe our preambles will keep this space safe—and keep us from facing our vulnerability.

But wouldn't that space be even more profound if you went in there once in a while? If you found a way to leverage your meaningful objects, memories, and vulnerabilities so they could do you some actual good?

Wouldn't that, then, be truly profound?

This isn't a self-therapy book. That's not my intent. Rather, I want to help you discover the three mysteries of profound space and see how they show up in your life.

Do you now know how courage can give you a gentle nudge to do what's necessary, no matter how hard? How can insight and its transformative impacts affect your growth and your future? How can autonomy help you develop meaningful direction, self-accountability, and eventually fulfillment?

Why is any of this important? Well, I have yet to meet someone who doesn't struggle with these mysteries daily. Lots of people are waiting around for confidence to just show up.

Lots of people think trivial information will get them ahead. Lots of people believe unfettered freedom is truly possible.

We all share in the mysteries of profound space. The mysteries are universal—and always will be, so long as the human species is confronted with fear, has imperfections, and desires fulfillment. Yet we all experience the mysteries in drastically different ways. That's what makes this *profound* space.

So, what will you do with your cigar box? You can leave it alone, allowing the objects inside to lie fallow. You can tell yourself they're just a bunch of meaningless objects, even if you don't feel like throwing them away.

Or you can create profound space with them.

The choice is yours. Because there is always something deeper.

Postscript: Profound (Work)Space

As important as profound space is to you personally, it's equally, if not exponentially, more powerful when applied to groups. Families that create profound space deepen their bonds. Teams that create profound space support greater communication, collaboration, and unity.

And workplaces that create profound space become more efficient, clarify their sense of direction, handle workplace anxiety with greater ease, and become psychologically safe environments.

On that note, let me tease you just a little about the future of profound space.

It's something we'll call profound (work)space.

And it's the answer to the current leadership ~~crisis~~ opportunity.

Let me explain.

Go online, and even a brief search will return you dozens, if not hundreds, of provocative testimonies describing a sudden "leadership crisis" in our corporations and organizations. According to these commentaries, the crisis is rooted in various sources—from insufficient leadership training to a generational power shift to a negative correlation between technology advancements and social skills.

I'm not here to sound the alarm on something that has been unfolding for multiple decades. For that matter, I don't believe any *crisis* is darkening our doorstep at all.

There are leadership gaps in our organizational structures, yes. But calling that a "crisis" is the exact form of pessimistic, fear-based leadership we need to get away from.

That's not profound space.

We need to do better. We need to see this not as a leadership *crisis* but a leadership *opportunity*.

Many proactive workplaces are already stepping up to meet this opportunity. They're investing in the health, growth, and development of their people in several ways:

- They're focusing on efforts such as corporate culture design; diversity, equity, and inclusion (DEI); professional development programs; and high-potential leadership paths.
- They're shifting away from a knowledge-based economy (what you *know*) and moving toward a skills-based economy (what you *do*).
- They're placing greater value in social and emotional traits and skills—especially with the recent surge in AI technology and the uncertainty it creates in the corporate landscape.

- Σ They're attempting to balance their workforce through the hybrid-work model, and they're seeking people-managers who can navigate the varied and vast challenges this presents.

As you consider those bullet points above, do you see what I see? That's movement toward profound space, right?

These forward-thinking corporations are beginning to create profound space—only they don't know to call it that, they don't have a clear framework for it, and they don't know what measurable outcomes they'll see from it. But they're inevitably responding to the complex landscape of the workplace with a new lens, seeking a new way.

Just think what these workplaces could do—what your own workplace could do—if they had a clear road map showing them how to create profound space in their organizations. Just think how workplaces could meet this leadership opportunity if they knew how and why to develop confidence through courageous action, build insight through personal transformation, and foster autonomy through self-customs.

Welcome to profound (work)space.

This is where my team and I are heading next.

So, follow our work at createprofoundspace.com. There you can learn about current and upcoming projects, you can complete the CIA Inventory to gauge your mastery of the three mysteries, and you can sign up for ongoing updates, events, workshops, and courses.

Maybe you'll discover ways that we can create profound space . . . together.

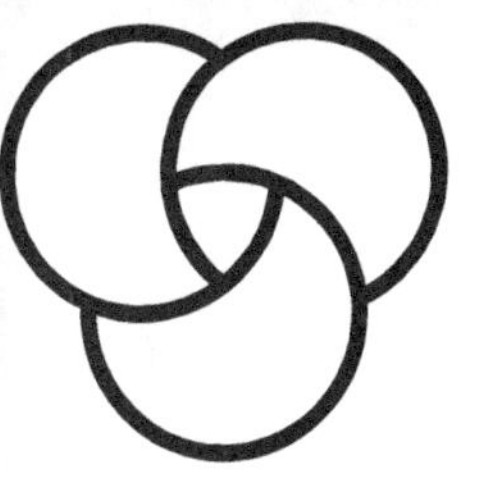

Acknowledgments

Accomplishing something alone is blindness.
True vision sees all those who helped you get there.

THE DEEPEST OF gratitude goes to my lover, my partner, my wife. **Sosha Brink,** your gentle patience, astonishing support, consuming love, and unwavering faith in me is like nothing I have experienced. That I deserve you remains a compliment too fresh to fully comprehend.

* * *

With reverent gratefulness for my grandma **Vera Bents,** on whose farm I learned more about life and from whose faith I've learned more about love than from all the teachers I have collectively encountered.

* * *

This book would have risked substantial insignificance if not for the brilliance of **Angela Wiechmann.** Immersion editor.

Visionary. Lassoer of loose ends. Creative partner. Angie, I truly cannot thank you enough.

***

I embrace a life-enhancing amount of appreciation for:

- Σ My teacher, my friend, my mentor, and more, **Randy Nielson.** Catching fish was never the goal, nor will it ever be. Not for you and me. The profound space we create remains not fully explored. May we keep creating it for many years to come.
- Σ Here's the deal, **Andrew Roth**—our coalesced curiosity may never reach the sidewalk's end, yet it regularly arrives at conclusions inebriated with both possibility, and joy. The outlet to capture our stories of this journey to Zoltar and back has yet to be established. But whatever party we host, it shall remain a party attended by common men.
- Σ I came to you first, **Chris Bye**, with the structure of this material. You never said I was crazy. You see only opportunities. Your mindset continues to be a beacon of truth to the collective landscape of entrepreneurship as a whole and to me as well. Someday, we'll create something crazy together. And it will be . . . crazy good.
- Σ Unknowingly and unintentionally, you curated profound space for me, **Jeffery Manderfeld**, at a time

when we both least expected it but perhaps needed it most. You widened my eyes when fear held them tightly shut. Your contagious confidence was infectious in ways unimaginable. *Thank you* is an inferior sentiment for my gratitude for your mentorship and friendship. Who I become will be a direct result of your influence on renewing my sight. La Familia.

- Σ The continual support, wisdom, love, and increasingly strong bonds from the greatest siblings I could ask for: **Angie and Artur, Ben and Beth, Andrew and Hillary**. Each of your lives is an inspiration to me uniquely. And each of you are impactful enough to me that riding a bike together would be both a joy-filled challenge and a miraculous feat of balance, patience, wisdom, and childish behavior. But I would do it with each of you. Together. Again and again.

* * *

For all those who encouraged me in big and small ways. Who read the words. Who challenged the ideas. Who soaked in the content.

- Σ The unquestioning confidence from **Gina Stangl**.
- Σ The excitement from **Andrew McPherson**.
- Σ The continual advice from **Graham Riley**.
- Σ The steady-stream consciousness from **Brian Stangl**.
- Σ The energy and guidance from **Kevin Lovegreen**.

Σ The encouragement to write anything at all from **Gerard Bents.**

And for those whose brief but impactful encounters have inspired me along this exploration: **Mentor Patrick Kiefert, Mentor Don Wisner, Captain Abraham Levy, Coach Katie Kroll, Coach Eric Mech, and the life and memory of Max Bents.**

Lastly, in the pursuit of resolving a few of life's great mysteries through *Profound Space,* I acknowledge that these are not the only mysteries that challenge us. Most certainly I have not resolved them all. Nor will I. As truth has it, there remain many mysteries yet unresolved. I fear that failing to acknowledge those with whom I share these unresolved mysteries would leave me incomplete and unreconciled as to the depth and magnitude of how much they truly contributed to the work of *Profound Space.* Therefore, to those who share these unresolved mysteries, I extend this: *The issue is never the issue. There is always something more.* Whether we discover it or not is yet to be seen.

About the Author

TRAINED IN PSYCHOLOGY, human behavior, and systems transformation, Gerd has established himself as a global expert in organizational change and leadership development. With over twenty-five years of service as an entrepreneur, coach, pastor, organizational consultant, real estate investor, and corporate professional, he has leveraged his vast experiences and research to develop the theory and practices of *Profound Space*.

Gerd enjoys helping organizations drive progress and growth by resolving the three mysteries that create profound space. He is a leader in thought *and* practice in multiple areas of organizational development, including leading systemic change, curating culture, coaching key leaders, developing intentional leadership, and galvanizing strategic direction.

He has also served as insightful counsel to hundreds of high-performing professionals, helping them develop what he calls *personal acumen*, the ability to become your best self in life and business. Gerd's coaching roster has included key leaders of Fortune 500 companies, CEOs, heads of teams, top financial advisors, West Point graduates, elected officials, pastors, physicians, and professional athletes and coaches.

Gerd lives in River Falls, Wisconsin, with his wife, Sosha. He has two grown children, a long list of life goals, and too many hobbies to count.